DATE		

Cambridge Poets of the Great War

Cambridge Poets of the Great War

An Anthology

Michael Copp

Madison • Teaneck
Fairleigh Dickinson University Press
London: Associated University Presses

Associated University Presses
440 Forsgate Drive
Cranbury, NJ 08512

Associated University Presses
16 Barter Street
London WC1A 2AH, England

Associated University Presses
P.O. Box 338, Port Credit
Mississauga, Ontario
Canada L5G 4L8

The paper used in this publication meets the requirements of the American National Standard for Permanence of Paper for Printed Library Materials Z39.48-1984.

Library of Congress Cataloging-in-Publication Data

Cambridge poets of the Great War : an anthology / [compiled by] Michael Copp.
    p. cm.
Includes bibliographical references and index.
ISBN 0-8386-3877-5 (alk. paper)
    1. World War, 1914–1918—Poetry. 2. Soldiers' writings, English—England—Cambridge. 3. English poetry—England—Cambridge. 4. English poetry—20th century. 5. War poetry, English. I. Copp, Michael.

PR1195.W65 C36   2001
821′.912080358—dc21   2001023287

For Christopher and Geraldine

Contents

Over There

Comradeship

Out of Battle

Loss and Remembrance

13

A Bitter Taste

After the War

Acknowledgments

I AM INDEBTED TO THE COPYRIGHT HOLDERS FOR PERMISSION TO reprint the following:

Material from *Heroes' Twilight,* by Bernard Bergonzi, 1965. Reprinted by permission of Constable & Co. Ltd.

Material from *Siegfried Sassoon: A Study of the War Poetry* © 1999 Patrick Campbell by permission of McFarland & Company, Inc., Box 611, Jefferson NC 28640.

"I saw them laughing once," "In that rough barn we knelt," "And if a bullet," "When the last long trek is over," from *Poems* by Alec De Candole, 1920. Reprinted by permission of Cambridge University Press.

"Harrow and Flanders" ("A Grave in Flanders") by R. Crewe-Milnes, from *The Harrovian,* February 1915. Reprinted by permission of Harrow School.

Material from *The Iliad* by Homer, translated by W.H.D. Rouse. Reprinted by permission of ITPS Ltd.

"Here dead we lie," from *Collected Poems* by A. E. Housman. Reprinted by permission of The Society of Authors as the literary representatives of the Estate of A. E. Housman.

"Here dead we lie," from More Poems from *The Collected Poems of A. E. Housman,* © 1964 by Robert E. Symons, copyright 1936 by Barclays Bank Ltd., copyright 1965 by Henry Holt and Co. Reprinted by permission of Henry Holt and Company, LLC.

"Battle Hymn," "Reims," "Youth and War," from *Poems* by Donald Goold Johnson, 1919. Reprinted by permission of Cambridge University Press.

Material from Johnston, John H., *English Poetry of the First World War.* Copyright © 1964. Reprinted by permission of Princeton University Press.

"A Night March," "Night at Gomonic," from *Macedonian Measures* by John Macleod, 1919. Reprinted by permission of Cambridge University Press.

18

Although every effort has been made to obtain permission from copyright holders before publication this has not proved to be possible in some instances. Any inadvertent omissions or errors will be rectified at the earliest opportunity.

Cambridge Poets
of the Great War

Introduction

THE IDEA FOR THE PRESENT ANTHOLOGY ORIGINATED IN A CHANCE discovery I made some years ago on a bookstall on Market Hill, Cambridge. This was an anthology of Cambridge poets published in 1921.[1] It included the work of forty-seven poets, seven of whom are women. Twenty-eight of them had already published at least one volume of poetry. The remainder had seen their work published in various local and national journals and publications. On reading that "twenty-five of the contributors were in residence at their respective colleges during the year 1920, and many of the remainder went down in the academical year preceding the outbreak of war" (Davison ix), I was prompted to explore its contents more fully. I hoped and expected to find a number of examples of war poetry. This indeed proved to be the case, as twelve of them (eleven men and one woman) had written war poems. In addition to these twelve names the present anthology includes work by a further thirty-eight poets with Cambridge connections. There are, therefore, fifty poets represented here, of whom seven are women.

The bulk of Great War poetry can be assigned to one of five categories:

1. *Nationalistic poetry*, which is often stridently jingoistic in tone, full of overblown rhetoric, enthusiasm for the War, abstract concepts, archaic language and prewar poetic conventions. Keynote example: Oswald Norman's "Casus Belli" (p. 71).
2. *Celebratory poetry*, which pays tribute to the courage and fortitude of the fighting men, praises the value of comradeship, or expresses love for another soldier. Keynote example: Henry Simpson's "Two Nights" (p. 153).
3. *Descriptive or narrative poetry*, which attempts to re-create and preserve the nightmare topography and suffering of the battlefields. Keynote example: Frederic Bendall's "The Blizzard" (p. 110).

4. *Elegiac poetry* that expresses grief for the dead. Keynote example: Charles Sorley's "When you see millions of the mouthless dead" (p. 209).
5. *Poetry of protest*, which expresses indignation, often in biting satire. Keynote example: Siegfried Sassoon's "Suicide in the Trenches" (p. 225).

The urge to respond to the experience of the Great War on a personal level was universal. Equally widespread was the demand for war poetry on the public level, and many publishers were quick to exploit this particular market. The most comprehensive bibliography of British war poets of the First World War lists 2,225 individual poets and 131 anthologies.[2] Inevitably, much of this vast outpouring was little more than doggerel written by amateurs. Thousands of serving men, and not only the educated officer class, committed their thoughts and impressions to paper, in diaries, sketches, and verse. Their motives were various: some wished to make a record of their experience of the War, some attempted to make shape and sense out of its formless, absurd chaos, some sought to memorialize it, and others wrote to protest against it. Much of the poetry was written during the war while men were recuperating from wounds in hospital, or while they were on leave. Remarkably, many private soldiers, in spite of the often adverse and appalling conditions under which they lived and fought, somehow found time to write in the front-line or support trenches. The young subalterns, apart from their social and educational advantages, usually had slightly better conditions—a little more space, a little more time, and a little more comfort. Others waited until peace came to write their poems. In addition to all these so-called "trench poets," back home in England the newspapers published poems written not only by soldiers but also by civilians, including many by women.

Many anthologies of war poetry have been published. Some of those published in the last two decades are still in print. Different criteria have been applied by each compiler in assembling these anthologies. For example, one focuses on the soldier-poets who were killed during the war.[3] Another treats a specific aspect of human relationships in the war, namely male-bonding and homoerotic feelings.[4] A third concentrates on the familiar and canonical war poets.[5] A fourth treats women war poets as an exclusive group in their own right.[6]

Taking the Cambridge connection as the raison d'être for the present anthology has enabled me to include noncanonical as well as major writers, women as well as men, prowar and antiwar poems, and older civilians as well as younger soldiers, sailors, and airmen. I have elected to include many poems without imposing restrictive value judgements on my choice. In so doing I am seeking to ensure that the selection will give a broad indication of the social and cultural ethos of the time as well as represent varying degrees of literary merit. Indeed this collection of First World War poems can be seen as an attempt on my part to reflect and represent as fully as possible the great variety of war poetry writing. It includes those poets unanimously accepted as belonging to the Great War canon, such as Siegfried Sassoon, Rupert Brooke, and, in spite of a sadly limited number of poems, Charles Hamilton Sorley. A number of so-called "minor" poets are included, among them Harold Monro, J. C. Squire, A. A. Milne, and Edward Shanks. Many of the other names are probably less familiar, and some even totally obscure and forgotten. All have connections with Cambridge of one kind or another. Many were members of one of the colleges, some went to school or lived in Cambridge, and others were related to university men.

The poems have been grouped thematically into ten sections, not all of equal length. It is not an accident that two of the longest sections are "Over There" and "Loss and Remembrance." The former contains poems that attempt to fix the experience of the war, and the latter contains poems in which the poet seeks to come to grips with the meaning of death. The predominance of these two themes needs no attempt at overemphasis on my part. They are the overriding preoccupations of all the war poets, and, between them, cover the bulk of all war poetry.

In all, eleven young poets with Cambridge connections fell in the Great War. Seven had already been members of a Cambridge college: Rupert Brooke, Ferenc Békássy, Alfred Ratcliffe, Donald Johnson, Robert Beckh, T. E. Hulme, and Vivian Pemberton. Three others, Alec de Candole, Henry Simpson, and Jeffery Day, had been accepted for admission to Trinity, Pembroke, and St. John's respectively, but were killed before they had the chance to come into residence. Charles Sorley had been a pupil at King's College School. We should also recall that the Hungarian Békássy was killed while fighting on the side of the Central Powers. The eleven Cambridge poets who died in the war, in chronological order of their death, are:

25 ·

Rupert Chawner Brooke (King's), d. 23 April 1915, aged 27.
Ferenc Békássy (King's), d. 25 June 1915, aged 22.
Charles Hamilton Sorley (King's College School), d. 13 October 1915, aged 20.
Alfred V. Ratcliffe (Sidney Sussex), d. 1 July 1916, aged 29.
Donald F. G. Johnson (Emmanuel), d. 15 July 1916, aged 26.
Robert H. Beckh (Jesus), d. 15 August 1916, aged 22.
T. E. Hulme (St. John's), d. 28 September 1917, aged 34.
Miles Jeffery Game Day (St. John's), d. 27 February 1918, aged 21.
Henry L. Simpson (Pembroke), d. 29 August 1918, aged 21.
Alec C. V. de Candole (Trinity), d. 3 September 1918, aged 21.
Vivian T. Pemberton (Sidney Sussex), d. 7 October 1918, aged 24.

The deaths of all these young men are recorded on their college war memorial. Their names appear, either inside or just outside their college chapel, on stone or wood panels or in a book of remembrance, along with all the other former college members who did not come back. The long lists of names on these somber memorials vividly convey the scale of the losses suffered. The total number of casualties for the University as a whole amounts to approximately 5,000, that is, 2,162 killed and 2,902 wounded.[7] This combined total of killed and wounded represents roughly one third of all the former Cambridge University men who served in the armed forces. The numbers of dead recorded on each college memorial are usually related to the size of the college at that particular time, as can be seen from the following three examples of a large, a medium, and a small college:

Trinity   —574
Pembroke   —258
Downing   — 35

The mass exodus of students from the university to enlist in the early years of the war had a drastic effect on the number of students in residence, which plummeted accordingly, from 1,178 in 1914 to 235 in 1916. Such a situation in which the University was virtually paralyzed and could barely function properly or sustain itself meaningfully as a thriving academic community was not repeated when it came to the Second World War. From 1940 to 1945 a planned system of deferment ensured that there was a gradual and controlled diminution in student numbers,

thus ensuring the student population did not collapse cata-
strophically all at once as it did in the First World War. If we
take just one individual college at random, in this case Jesus,
and look at its intake of new students each year, we see a sig-
nificant and typical reduction:

1913—31
1914—24
1915—12
1916— 7

The effigy of the young soldier depicted on the Cambridge War
Memorial that stands not far from the railway station is worthy
of note. He is there to represent the four categories of young men
who left the region to fight in the War. The inscription on the
plinth indicates that the dedication is TO THE MEN OF CAM-
BRIDGESHIRE AND THE ISLE OF ELY AND THE BOR-
OUGH AND UNIVERSITY OF CAMBRIDGE WHO SERVED
IN THE GREAT WAR 1914–1919. The bronze figure strides out
purposefully in the direction of the city center. He does not, how-
ever, call to mind a farmer's son, or an office boy, or a Fen man.
He is a strikingly handsome young man, seemingly the arche-
typal ex-public school boy and college student. This impression
is vindicated when we learn of the origins of this figure. The
statue is called *The Homecoming* and is the work of Robert Tait
McKenzie. The story of the fascinating and complicated process
of decision-making that led up to the present monument has
been thoroughly charted.[8] There were lengthy discussions on the
type of memorial to be adopted, the raising of the money in-
volved, and the eventual siting. Finally all disagreements were
resolved and the bickering ceased, and the result is what we see
today. One of those who served on the Lord-Lieutenant's memo-
rial committee, Arthur Shipley, Master of Christ's College and
University Vice-Chancellor, recommended that Robert Tait Mc-
Kenzie be entrusted with the design. After viewing examples of
his work the other members of the committee concurred. The re-
sultant unblemished, idealized figure is actually based on a cer-
tain Kenneth Hamilton, a student whom Tait McKenzie had met
when a guest of Shipley's at Christ's (Inglis 600).

The majority of the poems included here were written and
published either during or very soon after the war, that is, be-
tween 1914 and 1921. One notable exception is the single poem

that comprises the introductory section, "Premonition." Charles Hamilton Sorley's uncannily prophetic piece of juvenilia (or, at least, it can be read as such with the benefit of creative hindsight), "The Tempest," was written in about 1908 when he was twelve or thirteen and a pupil at King's College School.

The section "Early Days" begins with Oswald Norman's two sonnets. They are characteristic of much of the poetry written in the early months of the war, being enthusiastic about war in general, full of heroic rhetoric, archaic language, exhortatory formulae, and abstract concepts, what Hynes calls the "Big Words."[9] Norman's jingoistic poems were written immediately after war was declared on 4 August 1914. In them he introduces a series of capitalized words: "Freedom," "Duty," "Right," "Honour," and "Justice." War is addressed as "thee" and "thy." The only weapon mentioned, and an anachronistic and symbolic one at that, is a sword: "When Right unsheathes the sword"; and "Shall Britain's sword within the scabbard bide, / When Justice needs the sharpness of its blade?" These two sonnets, written by a man of fifty-one, it should be noted, are typical examples of this kind of prowar patriotic verse that appeared in newspapers in the early days of the war.

In her "Many Sisters to Many Brothers" Rose Macaulay gives expression to the feeling of frustration that so many women felt in their marginalized position during the war. Before the war as a young tomboyish girl in games of mock conflict she could match and even outsmart her brother. And in a roughhouse setto she could give as good as she got. Her role in wartime, however, is reduced to that of sitting helplessly at home condemned to knitting socks, an activity she regards as futile, while he is privileged to participate in a much more direct and active fashion.

The constant thread that runs through much of the war poetry is an all-pervasive English sense of Pastoral. This can be seen in John Lewis Crommelin Brown's "Dedication." It is an Edwardian version of Pastoral, the frequently found elements of which are golden summers, shady elms, village greens, thatched cottages, and slow-moving rivers. This is, of course, a privileged Pastoral. Dreams of peace and home were centered almost exclusively on the countryside, mainly it has to be said, on the countryside of the southern counties of England. It is rare to find any other region of Britain as a focus for nostalgia. Here the locus of nostalgic wish-fulfilment is the Sussex Downs, and the specifics are sun, clouds, bees, heather, woods, pools, birds, and stars.

28

The poet dreams of sharing this rural paradise once more with another, a "dear lad," someone with whom he can share these joys in silence as well as in talk. Thus the poem becomes the subtly oblique expression of a homoerotic relationship.

John Nicklin's "From Whitechapel" is taken from his *And They Went to War*. This slim volume contains pen portraits in verse of a mixed bag of volunteers, including a miner, a poacher, a scholar, and, in this particular poem, a ne'er-do-well from the East End. This man is presented as a particularly repellent sub-human specimen: "wolfish face," "fangs half snarling," "flaccid lips." His potential for redemption from a life of perpetual petty crime lies in his being accepted by the army and doing his bit in the war: "His whole life's squalor to retrieve." This little volume was published early in the war, in October 1914, and was possibly conceived as a propagandist means of demonstrating that the country needed all kinds of men to come forward and serve.

William Ewer's "1814–1914" is his response to reading Thomas Hardy's verse drama, *The Dynasts*, which treated the Napoleonic Wars. Ewer draws parallels with the Great War. Britain's political leaders persuaded men to fight against Napoleon, but the result on the continent was the reinstatement of reactionary regimes, and at home the repression of peaceful demonstrations for reform. In 1914 the same means were employed to persuade men to go to war. In both instances, a century apart, "Stern stupid Englishmen" marched cheerfully off to war, oblivious of the lessons of history. The poem, published in 1917, implies that the postwar situation is unlikely to bring about any progressive change for the betterment of society.

Aelfrida Tillyard's "A Letter From Ealing Broadway Station" is just that, a loose adaptation of a letter from her brother who was later to become a distinguished Shakespearean scholar and Master of Jesus College. She appears to sense the humor and irony of her brother's situation to a greater extent than perhaps he does. He is involved in the tedious task of guard duty at night. Just two things keep him awake during his boring vigil in the damp, misty murk: the deafening clatter of a passing train, and nostalgic thoughts of the comforts and relationships of college life. Only in the final lines does the brutality of real war intrude: memories (or secondhand reports?) of the burning of Antwerp and of the panic-stricken citizens. But now he too realizes how incongruous his present role is vis-à-vis the wider war, and comments:

29

Well, if I serve the Belgian nation
By guarding Ealing Broadway Station,
I'll guard it gladly, never fear.
Sister, good-night; the dawn is here.

Robert Beckh's "The Song of Sheffield" is a rare example of awareness of the fact that much of Britain consisted of a blighted industrial landscape rather than an idyllic rural one. Smoke-belching chimneys for once replace lofty elms. There is an ambiguity at the heart of the poem. Is the "martial devil" the tyrannical Moloch of modern industrialization inexorably bearing down on its working population, or is it the necessary heavy industry responsible for the production of death-dealing blows to be hurled against the soldiers of an enemy power?

Siegfried Sassoon's "Absolution" is very different from his later bitterly satirical protest poems. It was written during his period of officer training at Litherland, some time between April and September 1915. It was first published in the *Westminster Gazette* on 28 March 1916. Like the earlier sonnet sequence of Rupert Brooke this poem idealizes and romanticizes war as an ennobling and transcendental experience. Both poets wrote these poems before any experience of the reality of the war and its concomitant horrors. Sassoon's later reaction to this example of his early war verse was, "People used to feel like this when they 'joined up' in 1914 and 1915. No one feels it when they 'go out again.' "[10]

Edward Shanks's "The Old Soldiers" and "Going in to Dinner" are representative examples of the sort of typical reaction in light verse to the early days of training following enlistment. His "Drilling in Russell Square" is a rather more serious meditation, interweaving three strands of present, past and future: drilling in autumnal London, some idealized memories of the delights of prewar France and Germany, and the uncertainty of a grim future on the Western Front. An indication that this poem was written before any experience of real warfare is provided by his inclusion of "an Uhlan's lance" as being the single specified threat to his well-being.

In part 1 of "Officers' Mess" Harold Monro gives voice to the feelings of exclusion and inadequacy that many educated young men, artists, writers, and intellectuals, must have had when surrounded by bluff philistine hearties. Part 2 traces the awkward failed attempt to have a meaningful conversation with such men. The poet's feelings after this experience are a mixture of superiority, embarrassment, humiliation, frustration, and depression. The poem ends on an ominous note: all of those who had participated in such an unsatisfactory exchange are "men waiting to be dead."

Rupert Brooke's five war sonnets, *1914*, written during November and December of that year, were first published in *New Numbers*. Familiar though these poems are (some would say too familiar), they are as Bergonzi says, "not very amenable to critical discussion. They are works of very great mythic power, since they formed a unique focus for what the English felt, or wanted to feel, in 1914–15."[11] Although, as Geoffrey Matthews has pointed out, "Brooke . . . was committed to the cause of the ruling classes and surrounded by their watchful care" (a reference, presumably to the reading by Dean Inge in St. Paul's Cathedral of "The Soldier" on Easter Sunday 1915, shortly before Brooke's ironic death, and also to Winston Churchill's valedictory encomium), nevertheless, Brooke's appeal cut across all class boundaries and ensured that he would be widely read and not just throughout the early stages of the war. My father, who left the Welsh coalfields to enlist in the Royal Navy, received a copy of *1914 and Other Poems* from the parents of his best friend who died in the war. It is the twenty-sixth impression and came out in March 1919. Most modern critics and scholars concur in seeing these poems as having little to do with war, and much to do with Brooke's personal problems and self-dramatization: "Elegant, melodious, rich in texture, decorous and dignified in tone, the *1914* sonnets do not deal with war; they reveal a sophisticated sensibility contemplating itself on the verge of war."[12] Matthews goes further when he avers that "the five famous 'war sonnets' . . . are not war poems at all, except in the most accidental sense, but—to put it crudely—poems celebrating the export of English goods."[13] And Caesar finds "the equation of love and pain . . . entirely symptomatic of Brooke's sadomasochistic impulses."[14] It was almost impossible to ignore Brooke. In some of his contemporaries he inspired unqualified devotion and adulation, in others bitter anger and contempt, mainly because of the distorting lens that was turned on him after his death as the myth of Rupert Brooke was created. One response was to parody his best-loved poems. There are four examples of this form of reaction in this volume: Philip Bainbrigge's "If I Should Die be not Concerned to Know" (p. 216), Albert Tomlinson's "If I Should Die Just Bury my Flesh" (p. 216), part of Digby Haseler's "Stray Leaves" (p. 147), and "In Billets" (p.

148), Frederic Bendall's revision of "The Old Vicarage, Grant-chester." These pastiches range between the scurrilously irreverent and the apologetically affectionate. In many ways the most telling verdict on Brooke's *1914* poems comes in the form of a brief but penetrating and perceptive critique contained in a letter from the youthful Charles Sorley to his mother. In it Sorley underlines the major difference between his outlook and Brooke's. Sorley totally rejects the Big Abstractions and the Grand Gestures (see Appendix A).

It is in the section "Over There" that we will see most clearly how "The 'war poets' coped with dire experience in language, it is as simple and miraculous as that. It is not so much, or only, that their writing mediated between such experience and a desire to create literature, but that they made their writing in response to that experience."[15] The section opens with three poems by women. They project themselves in imagination into an arena denied them, the battlefields, the dead and wounded, the ruined towns and villages. Rose Macaulay's "Picnic" tells of an event that many civilians living near the south coast experienced when the noise of a particularly heavy bombardment in Flanders or northern France could be heard distinctly if the wind was in the right direction. The picnickers, presumably mostly, if not all, women and girls, react without overt displays of emotion:

> We did not wince, we did not weep,
> We did not curse or pray; . . .
> We did not shake with pity and pain,
> Or sicken and blanch white.

Their feminine world is a tightly bound one, circumscribed by society's convention that war was no concern of women: "And life was bound in a still ring." In addition the women have erected their own psychological barrier to protect and insulate themselves against the pain and anguish that knowledge of war's horrors brings:

> We are shut about by guarding walls:
> (We have built them lest we run
> Mad from dreaming of naked fear
> And of black things done).

The poet fears that eventually neither of these defences will hold and that she and her friends and relations will crack under the strain.

Fredegond Shove's "The Farmer" opens with a peaceful evening pastoral scene: ploughed fields, birds, gentle hills, and a farmer walking home. The poet, while fully aware of the distant war, "cannot see the dead, / And cannot see the living in their midst." As she watches the farmer she sees in a vision a vast army of:

> Wide hosts of men who once could walk like him
> In freedom, quite alone with night and day,
> Uncounted shapes of living flesh and bone,
> Worn dull, quenched dry, gone blind and sick with war.

Aelfrida Tillyard's "The Stones of Belgium" is a sequence of short fragments, in each one of which the spirit of the ruined structure speaks. A fortress, a gravestone, a cottage, a brothel, and a milestone are representative remnants of a destroyed civilization. The optimism of the last quatrain comes as a faint glimmer of faith in the surrounding darkness.

Kenneth Saunders apparently experienced battle conditions. However, his poems "The Three Crosses" and "Brothers" are shot through with a number of examples of pre-War conventions of archaic poetic diction: "riven with ruinous shard," "twixt," "that deed of ruth bore fruitage," and "when the morrow broke." In spite of the poet's undoubted sincerity they come over as an uneasy amalgam of passionate piety, sentimental heroics, exaggerated posturing, and cloying moralizing.

The first of Alex Corry Vully de Candole's poems, "I Saw Them Laughing Once," begins and ends with the gods on Olympus laughing at man's folly. The soldiers have reversed the normal life cycle by burrowing underground in the daytime and crawling furtively about at night. The second poem, "In That Rough Barn we Knelt," replaces classical mythology with Christian ritual. At a makeshift service in a barn the poet and his comrades take communion:

> In that rough barn we knelt, and took and ate
> Simply together there the bread divine,
> The body of God made flesh, and drank in wine
> His blood who died, to man self-dedicate.

Their meditation is brutally interrupted by the deafening crash of their own guns opening up on the enemy. The poet is painfully aware of the bitterly ironic contradictions in the position of the fighting man with Christian beliefs participating in a "just war":

> Strange state! when good must use (nor other can)
> The tools of ill, itself from ill to free,
> And Christ must fight with Satan's armoury.

The Christian believer caught up in war is confronted by irreconcilable opposites:

> The shell that slays, and Christ upon the tree,
> The love that died, and man that murders man!

The next four poems form a set of variations on the theme of Pastoral. Pastoral is under threat in Maurice Baring's "August, 1918 (In a French Village)," and in Martin Armstrong's "A Vision." Pastoral is a source of moral reinforcement in Martin Armstrong's "Going up the Line." Pastoral will possibly triumph once again in Henry Simpson's "Last Song."

A. E. Housman's short generalized elegy, "Here Dead Lie We," is in the abbreviated style suitable as an epitaph to be carved on a gravestone.

It is followed by Lord Crewe's more individualized lament for one soldier who has died in a specified place, "in the marshland, past the battered bridge." The poet muses on the possible career such a favored young man might have enjoyed until he eventually dies at a naturally advanced age. The poet wonders if this truncated life can possibly contain the essence of the man.

Humor in the First World War was widespread and took many forms: cartoons, sketches, jokes, and irreverent parodies of popular songs and even of hymns. The humor could be benignly waggish, bitterly sarcastic, or even shockingly scatological, and it was frequently black. All these forms of humorous expression run the inevitable risk of appearing dated and lacking in the comic force they once possessed. They were very much of their time and were mostly targeted at and appreciated by other serving men. Humorous poems run these risks of obsolescence even more strongly. The four examples of light verse that follow display varying degrees of survival value. "The Soldier's Cigarette," Robert Beckh's light-hearted apologia, indicates the importance that regular supplies of tobacco had for the troops, whether in the front line, in reserve, in training or on leave. A constant source of humor was complaining. In "Gold Braid" A. A. Milne adopts the language and persona of a cockney greengrocer who has a whole list of grouses to get off his chest. In Vivian Pemberton's "War Meditations" the grievances are those of a young subaltern struggling to cope with his many duties. His "The Song of a Sad Siege Gunner" adds another common target of grumbling resentment, namely the general staff, who were seen by all serving soldiers as out of touch as well as generally out of sight. The unflinching brutality of the final stanza comes as quite a shock after so much semi-serious jesting:

> I've heard the anguished stricken cry of strong men and of weak,
> I've seen the limbless try to walk, the jawless try to speak,
> I've seen brave men grow sick with fear and grovel in the dust,
> But never have I seen blood drawn with one good bayonet thrust.

Although the majority of war poetry is by soldiers, examples by sailors and airmen can be adduced, and they add another dimension to the war. Edward Hilton Young shows in "Mine-Sweeping Trawlers" that he is aware of how the role of seamen lacks the thrilling horror of trench warfare, but as "fishermen of death," garnering enemy mines, they play a key part in the prosecution of the war.

Jeffery Day's "North Sea" is particularly successful in conveying the dreariness, discomfort, monotony, and danger of convoy routine. The context is the early part of his service aboard a seaplane carrier.

In addition Day is probably the best of the war poets who wrote about the life of airmen. His later service began at an experimental airstation at Grain. "On the Wings of the Morning" illustrates how accomplished he is at conveying the physical and emotional sensations of flying: movement, sounds, visual information, and the stimulation felt by the pilot.

In "The Call of the Air" Day exults in his lofty viewpoint and feeling of superiority and elation, and produces an ecstatic paean to flying.

"Dawn" shows how Day and his fellow pilots disliked their enforced early morning flights. Rather than present himself as the heroic flying ace of conventionally mythical proportions Day prefers to be self-deprecating about his role:

> Yet every day we bold bird-boys
> clamber into our little buses,
> and go and make a futile noise
> with bombs and cusses.

35

Most of the trench-poets' verse comes from the battlefields of Flanders and Picardy, but the experiences of men in other sectors of the war cannot be overlooked. Two poems by Frederic Bendall report on aspects of the ill-fated Gallipoli campaign. In "Suvla Bay" the poet must avert his eyes from the safety of the islands he can see to the west and turn his eyes east to:

> The grave of hope—the death-place of desire— . . .
> The sombre-circled heights we could not win.

"The Blizzard" is Bendall's vividly portrayed eyewitness account of an actual event, namely the torrent of rainwater that swept down the hillside gullies, overwhelmed the trenches, and engulfed and drowned scores of men at Suvla on 27 November 1915. For the next two days a fierce blizzard raged and many more men suffered severe frostbite or froze to death. The storm and the freezing conditions killed 280 men.[16] Bendall points out to civilians back home how little of the truth of this catastrophe was conveyed by newspaper reports:

> My friends at home—at breakfast you saw a casual hint
> Of half a quarter of the truth in seven lines of print.

With John Macleod's "A Night March" we move to another inhospitable region, Salonica. As the Scottish soldiers march off through the night their pipers are accompanied by various night sounds: the barking of wild dogs, the croaking of frogs, and the high-pitched humming of mosquitoes. Macleod notes a further source of death here in Salonica that was not a threat when previously he served in France—malaria:

> Some shall see wounds and Scotland, some
> By the Struma waters shall lie in state,
> Stricken of fever or foe; for them
> The cannon shall thunder a requiem.

In the two quatrains of Stuart Bellhouse's short poem, "Two Mornings," he juxtaposes two contrasting scenes, one drained of all colour, "mist-hung, "cheerless grey," "leaden eye," haggard Day," the other glowing with rich color, "Green, orange, amethyst, and gold." The mixture of observed visual phenomena and impressions on the one hand, and the personification of the willows, dawn, day, and morning on the other produce an uneasy, incoherent effect.

In the first line of his "To Wingles Tower" Vivian Pemberton says, "I sit and gaze at Wingles." The tower is presumably the church tower. The rest of the poem contains a number of specific topographical references as the poet surveys a panoramic landscape at dusk: "fading sunlight mingles / With the smoke," "the rattle / Of the wheels of transport going up the line," "the long white trenches, / Waterlogged and full of stenches," "the trees all bent and battered, / Seared with scars where shrapnel spattered," and "ruined hamlets." The last stanza returns to Wingles tower which the poet says he has been staring at for ages. Whether this gaze forms part of his reverie or the official duty of an observer is not made clear. The last line comes as something of a surprise when the poet reveals he has been dreaming of another (gender unspecified):

> And sometimes I fell to wondering
> If I'd not been sorely blundering
> When I thought I knew the meaning of your smile.

Digby Haseler's "At a British Cemetery in Flanders" is a solemn lament for the ordinary soldiers. His phrase "pitifully unprepared / For the great agony of modern war" contains an echo of Frances Cornford's celebrated lines about the death of Rupert Brooke:

> A young Apollo, golden-haired
> Stands dreaming on the verge of strife
> Magnificently unprepared
> For the long littleness of life.

The first stanza of "No Man's Land" by Robert Beckh consists of the words of a young subaltern leading his men over the top on a night raid, giving them instructions, warnings and reassurance. The remaining stanzas alternate the officer's narrative viewpoint with further snatches of direct speech. The reference to "Grim Pluto, Stygia's overlord" exemplifies a characteristic of much of the verse produced by the educated officer class, namely references, quotations, and allusions drawn from their previous education in the classics.

Harold Monro's "Youth in Arms" is a touching lament in the homoerotic vein. In part one the poet likens the young man to David whose qualities he continues to represent. Monro portrays him "Leaning backward from your thigh / Up against the tinselled bar." Seeing him in his khaki uniform with his rifle the poet wonders "Where's your sling or painted shield, / helmet, pike or bow?" In this way he conflates the battle accoutrements of various historical epochs. Old men regretfully planned the battles, fully aware of how many young men would die. "Grey beards plotted. They were sad. / Death was in their wrinkled eyes. . . . for well they knew / How ungrudgingly Youth dies." Part one ends with the poet calling the youth "David of a thousand slings." In part four the poet observes the corpse of the young man, and notes that "the lovely curve / Of your strong leg has wasted." Many poems about the dead lying in or under the earth of the battlefield play on the idea of their blood and bodies as seed or manure for refertilizing the earth. "You are fuel for a coming spring if they leave you here; / The crop that will rise from your bones is healthy bread."

T. E. Hulme's "Trenches: St. Eloi" begins by describing the trenches at night. This is mostly objective description, apart from the epithet "desultory" and the simile "as on Piccadilly." Sandbags, fires, mess tins, dead horses, and the body of a dead Belgian soldier are the components of the scene. There follows a series of curt statements of fact:

> The Germans have rockets. The English have no rockets.
> Behind the line, cannon, hidden, lying back miles.
> Before the line, chaos.

The linguistic austerity and verbal compression of this poem are characteristic of Hulme's antiromantic stance and of the theory and practice of Imagism, the development of which was influenced to some extent by Hulme's thinking (the Imagists sought brevity, precision, and clarity, and shunned vagueness). In the final two lines the poet intrudes. His mind and everybody else's have become numbed. Thinking is limited and narrow in focus. Stoical resignation, not protest against or rejection of the war, is the only solution:

> My mind is a corridor. The minds about me are corridors.
> Nothing suggests itself. There is nothing to do but keep on.

Albert Tomlinson's "Ghost of the Somme" fuses the real and the phantasmagorical. The episode which Tomlinson himself witnessed concerns a man with appalling facial injuries who comes stumbling along a trench before collapsing and dying.[17]

Tomlinson used this incident as the source of this poem and a second, "Manslaughter Morning," on this occasion minus the supernatural element.

This section ends with a group of poems by Siegfried Sassoon. "The Death Bed" was written at home at Weirleigh in August 1916 after a spell of recuperation in Oxford. It marks a significant advance on "Absolution" (p. 78). The former glorification of war has been replaced by a subdued lyricism and passionate but controlled sincerity. The first six stanzas chart the dying soldier's gradual decline. There is a considerable amount of water imagery that probably reflects Sassoon's time spent on the Cherwell. Sassoon's note to his poem reads, "A memory of hospital at Amiens and a canoe on the Cherwell. Refused by the *Westminster* without comment." (Hart-Davis, 53) We should note that whereas the *Westminster Gazette* accepted "Absolution," it was the pacifist-inclined *Cambridge Magazine* that published many of Sassoon's more satirical antiwar poems. In the sixth stanza the viewpoint changes. The poet summons up compassion and seeks help in ensuring the survival of this young soldier. A further brief change of viewpoint has death personified announcing its arbitrary choice:

But death replied: 'I choose him.'

In the last three lines the narrator returns to say that this man's death is followed by silence and sleep. The poems ends with the continuation of the war:

Then, far away, the thudding of the guns.

"Foot Inspection" was written on 3 April 1917, and is included among Sassoon's diary entries.[18] The diary entries for that period indicate a march of twelve kilometres on 2 April and twenty-one kilometres on 3 April. Many of his company were utterly done in on this stage and Sassoon "covered the last lap trundling two of them in front of him, while another hung on to his belt behind. The Company Sergeant Major had to carry their rifles. Not one of the three stood more than five feet high. Even those who had marched under their own steam were suffering badly, as a foot-inspection revealed."[19] Sassoon thought a lot of the men under his command, as they did of him, and the sight of them suffering so severely from badly blistered feet produced this compassionate response. They had to march eight miles on 4 April and a further seven miles on 5 April.

"Prelude: the Troops" was written while Sassoon was at Craig-lockhart where he was being treated for shell shock. The first stanza is a remorseless accumulation of negatives: "dim," "gloom," "drizzling," "disconsolate," "sodden," "dulled," "sunken," "hag-gard," "hopeless," "despair," "desolation," "livid." In the second stanza Sassoon reveals his admiration and love for the men who "cling to life with stubborn hands," and "Can grin through storms of death." They leave behind them "safety, and the bird-sung joy / Of grass-green thickets" and make their way to the anti-landscape of the war:

> Sad, smoking, flat horizons, reeking woods,
> And foundered trench-lines volleying doom for doom.

The last stanza contains some of the most impressively sono-rous and noble lines in all Sassoon's war poetry. The overall tone and a couple of phrases in particular are somewhat reminiscent of Wilfred Owen: "some mooned Valhalla," and "The unreturning army."

"How to Die" was also written at Craiglockhart. It first ap-peared in the *Cambridge Magazine* on 6 October 1917, and was later published in his volume of war verse, *Counterattack* in June 1918. It is a vignette of trench life, and in the second stanza Sassoon sardonically subverts the stiff upper lip ethos:

> But they've been taught the way to do it
>   Like Christian soldiers; not without haste
> And shuddering groans; but passing through it
>   With due regard for decent taste.

"The Dug-Out" was written at St. Venant in July 1918, and it was Sassoon's final poem directly drawn from his personal expe-rience in the trenches. One of its strengths is that it is less em-phatic and less strident than some of his overtly angry poems. "The success of 'The Dug-Out' . . . derives from the tension be-tween subjective and compassionate feeling and also from judi-cious under-statement."[20] Sassoon informs us that "Counter-Attack" was written at Craiglockhart in 1917, and was based on an earlier draft dating from July 1916. It is one of his most vivid, photographically intense depictions of the chaotic and hideous world of the frontline trenches. The second section, lines 7–13, is unmatched for visualised horror in all Sassoon's war verse:

> The place was rotten with dead; green clumsy legs
> High-booted, sprawled and grovelled along the saps
> And trunks, face downward, in the sucking mud,
> Wallowed like trodden sand-bags loosely filled;
> And naked sodden buttocks, mats of hair,
> Bulged, clotted heads slept in the plastering slime.
> And then the rain began,—the jolly old rain!

Sassoon compels complacent civilians to confront the stark brutality of the war. In the last half of the poem we are presented with one soldier's predicament as he helps to hold the enemy trench against the inevitable German counterattack. Sassoon shows how men reacted like automata in such circumstances: "And he remembered his rifle . . . rapid fire . . . / And started blazing wildly." In the ensuing shambles he is hit by a shell. He does not die immediately, but "fought the flapping veils of smothering gloom." But soon, "Down, and down, and down, he sank and drowned." The word "drowned" has a triple function. It not only chimes with "down" but suggests his descent into final unconsciousness, and underlines the fact that he probably will drown in the "sucking mud" that fills the trench bottom. The laconic ending, "The counter-attack had failed" is characteristic of Sassoon. These emotionless words, typical of an official report, come directly after the powerfully narrated agonizing death of an individual soldier.

The poems in the section "The Enemy" reveal a generally sympathetic attitude towards Germany and towards German soldiers in particular. Among the trench poets a feeling of shared mutual suffering was commoner than one of hatred and revenge.

Charles Sorley's "To Germany," was almost certainly written during the first month of the war. He posted it home in April 1915, and it was first published in *Marlborough and Other Poems* in January 1916.[21] After leaving Marlborough, Sorley decided to spend some time in Germany before going up to Oxford. Part of this time he spent in a German home and later he was a student at the University of Jena. During this stay he became deeply sympathetic toward German people and German culture. He was called home when it became clear that war was inevitable. He was shocked by the mood of hysterical war fever that greeted him in England and strongly disapproved of the popular mood of simplistic jingoism. His sonnet demonstrates a remarkable awareness of history combined with a mature and reasonable humanity that is not found in any other of the war poets writing in 1914. Sentimental attitudes have no place in Sorley's outlook. The octet is full of blindness, tunnel vision, and narrow perspectives, whereas the sestet looks forward to an opening of eyes and minds. Cross admires the "attitudes expressed in that poem, [but] it has to be said that its impact is diminished by the euphemistic metaphor with which it ends—'But until peace, the storm / The darkness and the thunder and the rain.' "[22]

Ferenc Békássy's "1914" is written from the viewpoint of a Hungarian cavalryman killed in battle: "found rest / 'Midst the roar of hooves on the grass." Békássy himself was to meet such a death in a cavalry charge, a form of fighting that was swiftly to become a futile anachronism in an increasingly mechanized war. The landscape he refers to is, of course, not an English one, but somewhere on the Austro-Hungarian plains: "When the cow-herds answer each other and their horns sound loud and clear."

Henry Simpson's "Last Nocturne" is noteworthy for its economy, strong visuals, and choice of words that are predominantly monosyllables. These monosyllables produce an appropriately staccato effect to convey the sequence of flash images that fleetingly meet the poet's eye under the spasmodic sources of light during a night battle.

The informative detail at the beginning of John Brown's "The German Dug-Out" serves to underline the difference between the often shallow, hastily dug, and improvised British trenches and the deep, well-constructed and well-furnished German trenches. The detail of the black rub marks on the doorpost indicates the authenticity of the poet's experience. The poet imagines how the sixteen German soldiers lived down there under bombardment and wonders how exactly they died. There is neither triumphant gloating nor false emotion at the sight (and smell) of these sixteen dead German soldiers.

Albert Tomlinson's "To German Soldiers" was written in early 1918 and was first published in his volume of verse, *Candour*, in 1922. It is an angry poem, but the anger is directed not at the German soldiers whose tenacity in battle he grudgingly admires (in part 2), but rather, in part 3, at journalists and others eager to prolong the war. Part 4 suggests that the put-upon men of both sides will eventually rise up and take their revenge on those who subjected them to mutual massacre. The poem offers some features characteristic of a lot of Tomlinson's war poetry: a ponderous metrical line, verbal constructs (funkermen, fightermen, writermen, richmen), slang (miking) and a fondness for alliteration (khakimen curse only quitters, The sob of the soddish minny arrests not your sedulous spade). The strengths and weaknesses of such writing were properly evaluated by many early reviews and criticisms of Tomlinson's volume, *Candour,* which contains a number of war poems: "There are forcible lines in almost every poem, there are striking words, and there is imagination. . . . There is a feeling of too much straining after effect in the manner of these poems and in the words selected to express the author's thoughts. Nevertheless there is much evidence of power and the possibility of cultivation of gift" (Copp 74).

"Homoeopathy" is another example of light verse. Here, in response to newspaper reports of the activities of those who sought to express their anti-German feeling in mindless acts of petty, sometimes, violent, acts of vindictiveness, a couple of cockneys initiate their own ill-founded vigilantism. J. C. Squire's language approximates to the cockney accent and slang speech patterns of London working men:

> We was in the 'Blue Dragon,' Sid 'Awkins and me,
> When all of a sudden, "Here, Ernie," says he, . . .

In "Tom" Digby Haseler can barely restrain his mounting anger when he all but accuses German soldiers of a sadistic atrocity, that is, that they deliberately allowed a badly wounded British soldier to lie out in No Man's Land. The Germans, so Haseler believes, could and should have shot the wounded man and put him out of his misery, but they continued to let him cry out for water so that other British soldiers would crawl out to help him and thus get shot in the process.

Sassoon wrote "Enemies" on 6 January 1917. The idea of enemy soldiers meeting in Hell would later be more fully developed and more satisfactorily resolved by Wilfred Owen in "Strange Meeting." Thorpe argues that "though it is implicit in [Sassoon's] war poetry as a whole that he has no strong anti-German feelings, his failure to crystallise this into a positive attitude exemplifies his limitations" (Thorpe 33).

"The Effect," written in the summer of 1917, is Sassoon's bitterly expressed response to a war correspondent's bland summing-up of a visit to the battlefield to see the results of a heavy

British bombardment on German positions, "He'd never seen so many dead before." The "effect" that Sassoon wishes to convey is that death in war is not grand, noble or uplifting, but horrific and degrading. He employs a deliberately shocking image to portray Dick just before he dies, "Flapping along the fire-step like a fish." The final three lines in direct speech parody a street salesman's patter and serve to intensify Sassoon's angry sarcasm:

> 'How many dead? As many as ever you wish.
> Don't count 'em; they're too many.
> Who'll buy my nice fresh corpses, two a penny?'

In the section "Hope" a number of poets focus their thoughts on the future in a variety of ways.

In "Billets" Robert Beckh concentrates on the prospect of leave and a rural idyll.

In "Battle Hymn" Donald Johnson puts his faith in the sanative power of religious belief.

In "Reims" he seeks the rebuilding and restoration of a ruined historic monument, accompanied by just punishment of the guilty for such an impious act.

In his "Youth and War" he opposes Pastoral with war's depredation in anticipation of the former helping love to win through in spite of all the odds.

Strength to face death is Alec de Candole's wish in "And if a Bullet."

Alfred Ratcliffe longs for an end to war in "Optimism."

Iolo Williams would like nature in Flanders to simulate the English countryside for the benefit of the English dead that lie there ("From a Flemish Graveyard").

A. A. Milne's "From a Full Heart" is a characteristically jaunty piece of jokey wish-fulfilment full of nonsensical childlike fancies.

Digby Haseler's "Stray Leaves" is a sequence of jottings which includes a brief parodic reference to Rupert Brooke's "The Soldier," and ends with a plea for his own survival so that he can savor life's beauties once again.

Frederic Bendall's "In Billets" skilfully mimics Rupert Brooke's "The Old Vicarage, Grantchester," with some of the villages of the Western Front standing in for the Cambridgeshire villages of the original. This is yet another plea for a consolatory vision of returned Pastoral to conceal the ravages of war.

Sassoon's "Stretcher Case" is a further juxtaposition of Pasto-

44

ral and war. It was written in August 1916 at Oxford where he was recuperating from being wounded, and is strongly autobiographical. Gradually it dawns on the wounded soldier in his semiconscious daze that he is travelling by train through a late summer landscape. He strives to put behind him painful memories, "glooms and quags, / And blasting tumult, terror, hurtling glare." Eventually he realizes that he is alive, who he is and, finally, that he is in England. The clinching evidence for this awareness comes in the final four lines:

> Then shone the blue serene, the prosperous land,
> Trees, cows and hedges; skipping these, he scanned
> Large, friendly names, that change not with the year,
> Lung Tonic, Mustard, Liver Pills and Beer.

The poem was published in the *Westminster Gazette* on 28 September 1916. Given that this publication regularly and consistently rejected his more virulent antiwar poems, it is not difficult to see why the unruffled tone of this genial poem met with its approval. It was later included in *The Old Huntsman and Other Poems* in 1917. One reviewer, when considering these last four lines, wrote that Sassoon's realism was "of the right, the poetic kind. The real things are put in not merely because they are real, but because at a certain moment of emotion the poet happened to be struck by them and is not afraid of spoiling his effect by calling them by their right names."[23] It is perhaps surprising to learn that the reviewer who responded so positively to the poem's rather bathetic conclusion is the fastidious Virginia Woolf.

The section "Comradeship" contains poems about what was perhaps one of the most positive things to come out of the war, namely the bond that linked the soldiers in a platoon in a trench, the sailors in a mess room on a warship, or the pilots in a squadron. There was also the attachment and affection that many young officers developed for the men under them as well as for like-minded spirits among their fellow officers. These close relationships often, but not always, had homoerotic overtones. The introduction to one of the previously mentioned anthologies provides a perceptive and sympathetic study of this aspect of the war (Taylor 15–58).

Henry Simpson's "Two Nights" is another poem in mostly monosyllabic words (see also his "Last Nocturne" p. 128). The poet refers to his friend as "him" in the first stanza. They are walking and talking together at night when they hear someone singing. The poet recalls a past time when they were together. Now the other becomes "you." They stand together, in silence. The contact is now physical rather than verbal, "the touch of a warm hand." The poet twice expresses his anxiety about the other's safety, "(God! if he dies.)," and "(God! if he's dead)."

John Macleod's "Night at Gomonic" returns us once again to Salonica (see also his "A Night March" p. 111). The poem begins with another night scene, and the poet remembers the other "Who lived and laboured and laughed with me." In the central stanzas the poet lists a series of impressionistic details—place names, activities, landscape scenes, and sights and sounds, all of which he experienced and shared with the other. War is powerless to weaken or destroy the foundations of this relationship:

> In those days fury nor fear, let slip
> Tho' it were by hell, the delight could strip
> From youth's war-vanquishing comradeship.

In the first line of each of the four stanzas in "Outposts" Frederic Bendall asks the sentry what he saw, heard, did, and said. The poet replies that he saw nothing in No Man's Land by the light of a star-shell, then that his "mate" was hit by a bullet and killed. The sentry's final response at this loss of his comrade is one of revenge:

> I prayed the Lord that I'd fire straight
> If I saw the man that killed my mate.

The focus of Sassoon's "The Triumph" is not on one particular individual but the men he is responsible for. Once again we have Pastoral contending with war. In the first stanza the poet "sought for the triumph that troubles the faces of men" in a landscape of hills and glens. In the second he emerges out of the fear and despair of fighting to rediscover beauty once more:

> . . . and Beauty returned through the shambles of night;
> In the faces of men she returned; and their triumph I found.

In Sorley's "From an Untitled Poem" the "I" of the poet is absent, subsumed in a collective "we" whose energy and self-confidence are those of a unified body of men.

46

Albert Tomlinson's poems "Their Friendship was Mine," and "Men of the Line" were not included in *Candour,* and were not published until long after Tomlinson's death (Copp 75, 84–85, and 86–87). They are similar in theme and treatment. One is very probably a reworking of the other, although which preceded the other is hard to say. There are very few war poems that enumerate the social classes from which the ordinary soldiers came, but Tomlinson lists for us "Workman and farmer, shopman and clerk" in the former, and "ploughman" and "clerk" in the latter.

Geoffrey Fyson's "To a Fallen Comrade" mourns the loss of a very young comrade:

> You came to us fresh from school, bright-eyed,
>   With clear young voice that brought new zest
> To hearts grown sick with hope denied,
>   To limbs that were worn and craved for rest.

The poet calmly remembers the horror of his burial:

> And all that we could find of you,—
>   Of your white limbs, of your young frame,
> We gathered up into a sack
>   And bore to a quiet resting-place;

For him there will be no love of woman or children. Instead there was the reward of "The bonds of comradeship," and the affection of the men under him, "the blind worship of your men, / your dumb, proud followers to death." None of the meannesses of life will drag him down:

> No fetid life on office stool,
> Compassed with trivial compromise
> To clog your spirit, . . .
> Love that grows grey and turns to lust, . . .
> And Gods that crumble into dust.

In the first stanza of John Brown's "No Man's Land" the poet presents himself as a father seeking and finding his son killed in battle. The next two stanzas describe the men in the trenches at the end of a night's nervous tension, and the poet wonders at the absurdity of being required to kill fellow human beings while they sleep. In the fourth stanza the poet touches the boy's familiar features for the last time. The poet finally prays that God will either reinstate peace or destroy all the fighting men.

47

Rupert Brooke's "Fragment" is a late poem written in April 1915 while on his way aboard ship in the eastern Mediterranean to Gallipoli, and just before his ironically unglamorous and anticlimactic death from septicemia. On the evidence of this poem it is interesting to speculate as to how his poetry might have developed. It gives a tantalizing glimpse of a possible new direction with its closer attention to concrete detail, acutely observed.

The poems in the section "Out of Battle" deal with categories of people who are absent from the fighting for various reasons: they are women, they are wounded and recovering in hospital, they are dead, they are civilians, they survived and came home, or they were pacifists.

Vivian Pemberton was killed in October 1918 and his poem "An Only Son's Dying Lament" was published posthumously in his one volume of poetry, *Reflections in Verse*, in 1919. This poem is written from the viewpoint of a reluctant soldier, dreaming of past delights in England, who knows he is about to die and whose only wish just now is a drink of water to ease his raging thirst. This downbeat ending ensures that the incipient nostalgic romanticism of the earlier stanzas is put in its proper perspective.

During the war Rose Macaulay and Kathleen Wallace were both confined in or near Cambridge. Rose Macaulay's "Spreading Manure" springs from her experience of working as a volunteer on the land, on Station Farm just outside Cambridge. As she works in the mud, wind, and cold she begins to think of the similar conditions on the Western Front. As in her poem "Many Sisters to Many Brothers" (p. 72) she wishes she could be out there alongside the men, sharing their harsh conditions. She stoutly claims she could endure all these hardships, even death.

The setting for Kathleen Wallace's "Interval: Front Row Stalls" is a theater, in all probability the A.D.C. Theatre in Cambridge. The first three lines consist of impressionistic details of theatrical artifice and artificiality. During the interval she catches a glimpse of the newspaper that the man next to her is reading. She notes the summary headlines, a mixture of optimistic reporting, "three mile advance," and "we take the guns," and barely concealed hints of catastrophic casualties, "Bitter weather," and "heavy losses." In the final stanza she imagines that the seats between her and the curtained stage are filled once more by the young men students she once knew, many of whom now in all probability are among those killed in the reported battle.

Margaret Postgate Cole's "The Veteran" is all the more effective for being so understated. The poet and the young, blinded soldier have no illusions. Only the soldiers from the pub, yet to experience the fighting, have a faulty perception of what awaits them. At the conclusion we are given the soldier's age, nineteen, in response to the women's question, without authorial comment or intervention.

Digby Haseler's "In Praise of Nurses" is another poem by a wounded soldier lying in hospital. For the most part immobile and with little to occupy their time, many young men spent their period of recuperation writing verse. The tone is light throughout. There is no mention of wounds or suffering, either physical or psychological. It is a love poem addressed to all nurses. The inclusion of literary, classical, historical, and biblical allusions and references gives a clear indication of the kind of education that many young men of Haseler's generation received.

Geoffrey Fyson's "The Survivors" is a defiant cry of pride on behalf of himself and fellow survivors and a promise never to forget the dead. The language is euphemistic and old-fashioned in places, "stretch'd quivering on the rack," and "leaves of coronal . . . heaped upon our brows."

His "To a Pacifist" is an assault couched in virulent hyperbole, "You, with your turgid soul and venomous tongue," and "A saprophyte upon the sepulchre, / Lapping the spilt blood of the crucified." His anger appears to be directed more against those who were vociferous publicists against the war, rather than on those more quietist souls who went uncomplainingly to jail for their beliefs. The "big words" are important to Fyson: "Honour" and "Death."

A number of the poems in this anthology contain visionary episodes. For example, in "The Army of the Dead" Barry Pain dreams of British and German soldiers marching together across the sky, all of them whole, unblemished, and free of destructive passion. This is yet another war poem expressed in archaic language and obsolete imagery:

> Beyond these tangled spheres
> The Archangel's trumpet calls;

The subject of John Brown's "In Montauban" is not the customary dead young soldier, but a much older man in his sixties, probably a member of a Pioneer Battalion, and one who volunteered to come out to perform menial tasks of work such as trench-digging. The poet imagines him as he was, working as a gardener in England (again there are pastoral elements by way of contrast: cottage, sun, flowers, bees). It is now the poet's turn to dig, that is, to dig a grave for the old man and lay him in it.

Owen Seaman's "The Soul of a Nation" illustrates how a generalized hortatory message of imperialistic patriotism, expressed in portentous language ("O England, staunch of nerve and strong of sinew"), and stale clichés ("our hearts are straining") could still be written at such a late point in the war, that is, March 1918.

"Bridging the Gulf; or, The Union of Classes" is J. C. Squire's lampoon of the privileged, remote and out of touch upper classes attempting to tighten their belts and do their bit. The humor and running meter are well sustained throughout. This is possibly one of the most successful humorous poems to come out of the war.

Part of Tomlinson's "War" has much the same target as the previous poem but the means employed are very different:

> For babes that are born to Rolls-Royces will grow bellyslackly
> to hogs,
> And wax on éclairs and harlots to the crispness and candour
> of dough,

The harsh, angry blows of Tomlinson's satire have a crudely bludgeoning effect and contrast vividly with the controlled elegance and well-timed thrusts of Squire's rapier.

There follow Sassoon's two autobiographical poems written while he was at Craiglockhart. Both convey his anguish and turmoil as he contemplates his absence from his men. "Banishment" is the weaker of the two. It is marred by one or two infelicitous phrases, for example, the antiquated rhetoric of "They went arrayed in honour," and the weakly euphemistic "sent them out into the night." The forgiveness that Sassoon seeks and anticipates is forgiveness for his protest, "and mutinous I cried / To those who sent them out into the night" (see Appendix B). Sassoon trusts that his men will understand that his protest was made on their behalf to preserve them from pointless slaughter. Quinn is correct in defining the poem as "a sublimated love poem in praise of the soldiers who are still fighting and dying on the western front." [24] The restraint, controlled emotion and simplicity of "Sick Leave" make it a more effective and a more satisfactory poem than "Banishment." At the end of the octet Sassoon's feeling of guilt is expressed in the question that he imagines is being asked by his men:

> 'Why are you here with all your watches ended?
> From Ypres to Frise we sought you in the Line.'

The oxymoron of "bitter safety" comes as quite a shock, given the comfortable physical conditions of life at Craiglockhart. The bitterness comes from the guilt that Sassoon inflicts on himself. The sestet ends with the questions Sassoon asks himself:

> 'When are you going out to them again?
> Are they still not your brothers through our blood?'

This section ends with the "Letter to Robert Graves (Dear Roberto)." This poem is rarely if ever anthologized, and is frequently ignored or given little more than a cursory mention in many studies of Sassoon's war verse. Campbell, however, argues persuasively that it is "one of the key poetic documents of Sassoon's war."[25] Its "expressionistic procedures," "erratic content," and "associative leaps" (Campbell 1999, 192, 193) are evidence of Sassoon's highly wrought state as he lay recuperating in a London hospital. The "deathly verses" refer to his poem "I Stood with the Dead" which had recently been published in the *Nation* on 13 July. In the third stanza mention is made of visits made by various friends: Eddie Marsh whose flat in Half Moon Street was a meeting place for many writers and artists, Roderick Meiklejohn, Robert Nichols, whose first book of poems was *Ardours and Endurances*, and Osbert Sitwell. After these over-stimulating visitors the calming presence of Dr. W. H. R. Rivers, who treated Sassoon at Craiglockhart, assuaged his fraught nervous state. There is a sharply couched rhetorical question about obtaining money from a Jew. Graves was in the habit of borrowing money from Sassoon, and we should recall Sassoon's half-Jewish origins. "Jolly Otterleen" is Lady Ottoline Morrell, at whose house, Garsington Manor, Sassoon had been a frequent visitor. Sassoon refers to himself in self-deprecating but quite accurate and appropriate terms: "the wonderful and wild and wobbly-witted sarcastic soldier-poet," and "Dotty Captain." "Dotty" is Sassoon's shorthand for his brittle mental state of nervous exhaustion, but also recalls the nickname he coined for the hospital at Craiglockhart—"Dottyville" ("Sassons," which is used at

51

the end of the letter/poem, was one of Sassoon's army nick-
names). There follow two references to popular songs of the day:
"You made me love you: I didn't want to do it" and "God send you
back to me." The letter/poem ends on an abrupt note of flippant
bathos which "in the light of the tormented paragraphs of the
rest of the poem, carries no conviction whatsoever" (Campbell
1999, 194). When Graves printed this "merciless piece of self-ex-
posure, . . . assuredly *not* intended for public consumption" in an
altered form in the first printing of *Goodbye to All That* it "un-
dermined one of the most creative friendships of the Great War"
(Campbell 1999, 194–95).

It will not come as a surprise that many of the poems in the
section "Loss and Remembrance" are written by women.

In "Cambridge in Wartime" Florence Hobson notes with regret
the empty college courts, vacated by so many student volun-
teers. This poem was published in the *Cambridge Magazine* of
27 May 1916.

Next comes a sequence of five poems by Kathleen Wallace, née
Coates, "Chestnut Sunday," "Walnut-Tree Court," "Yesterday,"
"Died of Wounds," and "Unreturning." These poems of loss are
simple, restrained, dignified and very moving. They refer to her
brother, Basil Montgomery Coates. He was a former student of
Queens' College and his name appears on the memorial board in
the College Chapel. There are a number of topographical refer-
ences to Cambridge, the town, the colleges, and the countryside
around. For example, Walnut-Tree Court is part of Queens' Col-
lege where her father was Bursar and Assistant Tutor.

Rose Macaulay's "The Shadow" was written while she was
working at the War Office in London. Earlier in the war she had
worked on a farm on the edge of Cambridge (see her "Spreading
Manure" p. 168), and also had experience of working as a V.A.D.
nurse at a military convalescent home on the Gog Magog hills
just outside Cambridge. There are references to air raids in Lon-
don, searchlights, bomb damage, and death. Macaulay's mind
moves from the corpses buried in a previous raid to the "Plain
where limbs and dreams and brains to set the world a-fire / Lie
tossed in sodden heaps of mire."

Sassoon's "The Hero" first appeared in the *Cambridge Maga-
zine* on 11 November 1916, and was later included in *The Old
Huntsman*, published in May 1917. According to Sassoon it
"Does not refer to anyone I have known. But it is pathetically
true. And of course the "average Englishman" will hate it."[26]
Sternlicht sees the poem as "an excellent example of the emo-

tional ambiguity that resides behind Sassoon's war poetry." He calls it "a satire of circumstance, both sardonic and sentimental."[27] In the first stanza the mother's words of reaction to the news of the death of her son Jack brought by a fellow officer, are simple and conventional: ' "Jack fell as he'd have wished" ', ' "The Colonel writes so nicely" ', ' "We mothers are so proud / Of our dead soldiers." ' She manages to hold herself together emotionally. In the second stanza we learn that the visiting officer had "told the poor old dear some gallant lies." While relating this falsified version of events he felt embarrassed and guilty: "he coughed and mumbled." In the third stanza we are given the benefit of the visiting officer's thoughts. He calls Jack a "cold-footed, useless swine," who on one occasion "panicked down the trench," and on another "tried to get sent home." Finally Sassoon concludes the poem with, "And no one seemed to care / Except that lonely woman with white hair." Sassoon appears to be pulled in two directions. He feels for the mother's gullibility in being obliged to play her role in this manner; he feels for the colonel who is obliged to be economical with the truth; he feels for the visiting officer with his unpleasant task. He also is exasperated that the system demands such falseness from all concerned. What does Sassoon himself think about Jack? If he feels compassion for this shell-shocked individual we may possibly infer it but it is not really hinted at, let alone overtly expressed. We could be forgiven for thinking that Sassoon possibly shares the same condemnatory view as the visiting officer. It would not be until 1917 that Sassoon had direct personal experience of shell shock or neurasthenia and could appreciate the reality and true nature of this pathology.

In "Praematuri" Margaret Postgate Cole contrasts the attitude of old men and young people to losing their friends. The former "are not so sad" for various reasons: "their love is running slow," "they are happy with many memories," and they have "only a little while to be alone." But for the poet's generation their "memories are only hopes that came to nothing," and "there are years and years in which we shall still be young."

Her "The Falling Leaves" makes the comparison between leaves falling, snow falling and men falling in battle with simple directness.

In "Afterwards" the pleasures of living, lying on a hillside surrounded by trees, eating strawberries and cakes, delicacies that friends dangle temptingly and consolingly before her, are rejected by the poet. As it turns out, Nature is not consolatory. All she can see is woodland decimated, to make pit-props for coal mines and hence support the war effort. A pit-prop replanted would not grow like its original tree. In the last stanza the poet likens her dead lover buried somewhere underground to a pit-prop. So, having his body lie next to hers would be equally futile. The trees are "corpses of the larches / Whom they slew." "Corpses of the larches," of course, and the "red manes" of the larches in spring evoke the dead lying out on the blood-soaked landscape of war. And finally (though the poet is probably unaware of the military pun behind her words), "sap making the warm air sweet," if transferred to the world of the trenches, significantly alters in meaning. A "sap" is a shallow trench, and rotting corpses have a sickly sweet smell.

Ada Harrison's "New Year, 1916" is couched in outmoded terms: for example, phrases such as "garnered them no glory," and "The very dust is clamorous with their praise"; also there are two capitalized abstractions, "Grief" and "Renown."

Her poem, "The Poppies That Drop as I Watch," employs that familiar symbol for the death of soldiers, namely fragile poppies losing their petals.

In the next two poems John Brown addresses a dead friend. In "Missing: Unofficially Reported Killed" he has no direct, first-hand knowledge of the death, just an unconfirmed report.

In "The Dead Lover" the poet confronts his friend's corpse, imagines he can see him, though he is buried, and addresses him directly. This is another poem that utilizes the image of the dead fecundating the soil, "The young grass has its roots in you, your bones and members sprout." Homoerotic feelings are unambiguously expressed, as the poet remembers "your crisp delightful hair."

Henry Simpson's "Casualty List," written in *vers libre*, blends resentment at the irrelevant chatter of other people, memories of the dead friend, and anger at the waste of a life. The only color to enliven the overall mood of drab greyness is the red in the gleam of firelight that opens and closes the poem, although at first it is "Like the red heart of pity," by the end it is "like a fierce threat." Red appears in the middle section as "a splash of blood." Otherwise the poet experiences "misty drifts of words," and says of the other that "his life was grey" and full of "grey little pleasures."

In "The Grudge" Gerald Bullett rejects Binyon's attitude. He declares that he most certainly *does* begrudge the extinguished lives, for which loss there is no consolation to be found in fine phrases and high-minded attitudes:

> But our grief is naked and shivers, and will not be soothed
> By splendid phrases, or clothed in a moral glow.

Arundell Esdaile's brief "On a War-Worker" reminds us in the first two lines that soldiers perished not only in the mud of Flanders, but also in the very different desert landscape of the Middle East. The final three lines serve as an epitaph for a war-worker, a woman who has met her death in voluntary work on the home front. The nature of her work and the cause of her death are not specified. Thus Esdaile makes her into a universal, generalized figure, a representative of all such women, an "unknown war-worker" to complement the "unknown warrior."

Frank Sidgwick wonders in "The Dead" if he is compensating for the death of his friend by eagerly exaggerating his appreciation of the world's beauty.

In the sonnet, "The Halt," it is not made explicit if Edward Shanks is remembering dead comrades or just simply wondering where they are and what they are doing now he is not with them. The octet begins with the barked commands as the company stops to enjoy its ten-minute break after a fifty minutes march. The officers sit and watch their men and overhear snatches of their talk, "You weren't ever in step—The sergeant—It wasn't my fault— / Well, the Lord be praised at least for a ten minutes' halt." Only the poet is aware of the wider landscape. The sestet is a series of five questions addressed to the company. The poet imagines them halting in the midst of a landscape of hedges, poplars, and a sky filled with smoke, while they stamp their feet and readjust their loads before "looking with wary eyes at the drooping weather." We infer it is not the weather that they are worried about, but that it is their spirits that are drooping as they draw near to the battlefield.

E. Hilton Young remembers the dead sailors in "To the Boys Lost in Our Cruisers."

In "Return" he transfers memories of his dead friend onto the landscape that they planned to enjoy together. The dead man exists as a kind of pantheistic presence in nature, but not even that strongly experienced sensation can stop the poet's "thoughts from wandering to your unknown grave."

Guy Pocock's "Years Ahead" stresses that dead sailors, unlike the majority of dead soldiers, lack a clearly identifiable grave site.

In "Lament in 1915 (B.H.W.)" Harold Monro summons up a dead friend and imagines him knocking at his door and entering to pick up the threads of their former relationship. The poet's fervent anticipation and anxious wish-fulfilment are conveyed in short, urgent, exclamatory sentences:

> Don't make me angry. You are there, I know.
> Is not my house your house? There is a bed
> Upstairs. You're tired. Lie down; you must come home.
> Some men are killed . . . not you. Be as you were.

At the end sober bleak reality intrudes:

> And yet—Somehow it's dark all down the stair.
> I'm standing at the door. You are not there.

"Elegy" is a more subdued variation on the previous poem. Here Edward Shanks's optimism is muted and restrained in comparison with Monro's breathless eagerness.

Siegfried Sassoon's "The Last Meeting," written in May 1916, is a lengthy elegiac poem awash with romantic mysticism. In parts 1 and 2 the poet seeks a younger friend, a certain David Thomas, who was killed on 18 March 1916 (Sassoon was obviously infatuated with Thomas; he appears in two other poems, before his death, in "A Subaltern," and, after his death, in "A Letter Home"). The search takes place first in a ruined house and then in Nature. The weakness of Sassoon in this vein is neatly caught by Thorpe who writes that "he chooses a lush romantic style that smothers both the subject and some strong atmospheric description beneath a spurious richness of language" (Thorpe 31). There is an ambiguity about the final line, "And youth, that dying, touched my lips to song." "Touched," one feels, is meant to be read as "inspired," but also hints at intimate physical contact.

In "In Memoriam F.," his short elegy to a lost friend, Iolo Williams replaces the reality of sociable friendship with the power of vividly retrieved memories.

John Brown's valedictory tribute, "Rupert Brooke," is filled with light, optimism, idealism, and faith. The final three lines of the sestet remind us that Brooke's solitary grave is set on the Aegean island of Skyros.

The brief poem, "In Memoriam S.C.W., V.C.," first appeared after Sorley's death, in *The Marlburian*, 24 November 1915. The dedicatee was Sidney Clayton Woodroffe, a contemporary of Sorley's at Marlborough. He was killed in action at Hooge on 30 July 1915 and was awarded a posthumous V.C. (Wilson, 1985, 92).

The manuscript of "When you see millions of the mouthless dead" was found among Sorley's possessions in his kit after his death. It is reasonable, therefore to suppose that it was the last war poem he wrote. In it he ruthlessly deflates zealous remembrancers with their consolatory message and conventions of mourning:

> Say not soft things as other men have said,
> That you'll remember. For you need not so.
> Give them not praise. For, deaf, how should they know
> It is not curses heaped on each gashed head?
> Nor tears. Their blind eyes see not your tears flow.
> Nor honour. It is easy to be dead.

Line ten, " 'Yet many a better one has died before.' " is a paraphrase of a line in the Iliad, "Patroclos died too, and he was a much better man than you" (xxi, 107).[28]

The section "A Bitter Taste," begins with Aelfrida Tillyard's piece of gentle whimsy, "Invitation au Festin." In it she pokes fun at the reduced quality and quantity of food as recommended by the authorities to avoid squandering valuable supplies in wartime.

In "The Survival of the Fittest" J. C. Squire takes exception to a thoughtless statement reported in the press. With caustic irony he demolishes Tomkins's nauseating apologia for the beneficial effects of war, "without war the race would degenerate." The men who died did not see:

> . . . the war as a wise elimination
> Or a cleaning purge, or a wholesome exercise,

Squire claims they were seduced into the war by falseness and lies:

> Romance and rhetoric! Yet with such nonsense nourished,
> They faced the guns and the dead and the rats and the rains,

Geoffrey Young's "Waste" envisions men enslaved by the economic demands of war, "Grub for gold," "Dig the gold," "Drain the gold." This will help "rouse the brute in man" so that he becomes "Flunkey to a nation's pride / In the lust of fratricide."

Of the two parodies of Rupert Brooke's "The Soldier" in this section, Philip Bainbrigge's "If I should die, be not concerned to know" is more genial and lighthearted than Albert Tomlinson's "If I should die. . . ."

The section ends with a group of poems by two poets, Albert Tomlinson and Siegfried Sassoon, whose poems of protest are among the bitterest and most sustained assaults on various aspects of the war. In "The Strand 1917" Tomlinson adopts an extremist stance with his puritanical censure of metropolitan immorality. He expresses his disgust in virulently abrasive language (and a display of uncomfortable anti-semitism):

> A liquorous, lecherous pervadement of stench;
> body-stench with a frangipani dash.

Only in the final two lines does Tomlinson abandon his hectic and extravagant mode for a nonemphatic laconic ending in the manner of Sassoon:

> And very soon, the latest news of a week-old
> trench-raid is on the streets.
> The casualty-list to follow.

In "A Hero" Tomlinson's target is older civilians, and the generation of the poet's father in particular. The poem consists for the most part of a series of rancorous exchanges between the father and son before the latter goes off to war. He loses an arm in the fighting but returns home to work in a bank. Life could be worse, he concludes ironically:

> I lack a limb but got my keep.
> Besides I've got a decoration;
>
> I'm grateful to my pater's nation.

"Sed Miles" is arguably Tomlinson's most successful antiwar poem. The lumbering meter of "The Strand 1917" is replaced by a more springy, lilting rhythm. The satirical intent is just as powerful. The title would appear to refer to lines from Sir Henry Newbolt's poem, "Clifton Chapel": "Qui ante diem periit: / Sed

58

miles, sed pro patria" (Who died prematurely, but as a soldier and for his fatherland).

The seven poems that follow are some of Sassoon's most scathing antiwar poems. The compact brevity of these poems makes their impact all the more persuasive and forceful.

' "They" ' contrasts the Bishop's vaporous consolations of the first stanza with the colloquial directness of the troops in the second stanza. Sassoon gives the Bishop the final word, but his deplorably evasive theological platitude, ' "The ways of God are strange!" ' is left hanging ineffectually in the air without the need for further protest or comment. Sassoon tells us that when he wrote it (31 October 1916), "I was so sleepy I could hardly keep my eyes open, but the thing just wrote itself. And Eddie Marsh, when I showed it to him one wet morning (at 10 Downing Street!), said: 'It's too horrible.' As I was walking back I actually met 'the Bishop' (of London) and he turned a mild shining gaze on me and my M.C." The poem appeared first in the *Cambridge Magazine* of 20 January 1917, and later that year in *The Old Huntsman* (Hart-Davis 57).

"Blighters" was written on 4 February 1917 in response to an offensively jingoistic revue that Sassoon had seen at the Hippodrome. In the first stanza the theatrical scene and performers are presented in expressionistically caricatural terms. The audience "grin and cackle at the show," and the dancers are seen as "prancing ranks of harlots." In the second stanza Sassoon bitterly imagines an incongruous tank invading the fatuous vaudevillian inanities, before he undercuts the preceding artificiality with his stark reminder in the final line of "the riddled corpses round Bapaume."

"Base Details" was first published in the *Cambridge Magazine* of 28 April 1917, and later in *Counter Attack* in June 1918. The title contains a double pun: "base" suggests ignoble and menial as well as military headquarters; "details" conveys the idea of facts as well as of a military detachment. The staff officers are "scarlet," not only because of their red-tabbed uniforms but also, no doubt, because of their port-induced complexions. Their unthinking attitude to heavy losses is to refer to the last catastrophic battle as occurring in "this last scrap." Finally, in contrast to the men who have gone "up the line to death," the staff officer will be able to go home and die a natural death in bed.

Sassoon wrote "The General" while recuperating in Denmark Hill Hospital in April 1917. The eponymous officer greets the troops jauntily, "Good morning, good morning!" After this first line Sassoon adopts the collective persona of the body of men, and incorporates fragments of colloquial language: "most of 'em dead," and "slogged up." Two soldiers are named, but they have no specific individuality. "Harry" and "Jack" suggest they could be any Tom, Dick, or Harry. Harry's comment on the general, "He's a cheery old card" is cleverly ambiguous. Harry may be mildly amused, irritated, contemptuous, or sarcastic. A feature of many of these satirical poems is the final punch line, which in this instance is given emphasis in two ways. Firstly it is separated by a gap from the preceding lines. Secondly the general is stated as having been the cause of the deaths by the use of a telling euphemism. Instead of "slaughtered" or "murdered," Sassoon writes, "But he *did for them* both by his plan of attack" (my italics).

"Does it Matter?" is another Craiglockhart poem which appeared in the *Cambridge Magazine* on 6 October 1917, and subsequently in *Counter-Attack*. Each verse outlines the fate of three victims of the war: an amputee, a blinded man, and a case of mental breakdown. Each time the question, "Does it matter?," is put concerning each man's predicament, the answers and solutions offered by unscathed civilians are strikingly callous. The final line is the most heartless response of all, "And no one will worry a bit."

"Glory of Women" was written while Sassoon was at Craiglockhart and was published in the *Cambridge Magazine* of 8 December 1917. It is a scathing assault on women, and Sassoon enumerates a whole range of attitudes and reactions he regards as hypocritical and contradictory before reaching the point where he confronts these women with the stark reality of soldiers in war, "Trampling the terrible corpses—blind with blood." Then comes an abrupt switch to an expression of compassion for one group of women, namely the mothers of the dead German soldiers who have been trampled upon:

> O German mother dreaming by the fire,
> While you are knitting socks to send your son
> His face is trodden deeper in the mud.

This unforeseen display of compassion is not quite sufficient to dispel the uncomfortable feeling that the misogynous vilification of the first nine lines is overly harsh and unbalanced.

"Suicide in the Trenches" was published first in the *Cambridge Magazine* on 23 February 1918. In the first two stanzas

60

Sassoon's narrative proceeds in a straightforward, unemphatic manner. In the early days the young soldier "grinned at life," "slept soundly," and "whistled early with the lark." Later in the appalling conditions of the front line trenches in winter, "crumps and lice and lack of rum," he became "cowed and glum," and ended up by committing suicide. In the final stanza Sassoon rounds on the "smug-faced" civilians who urge men on to fight. He tells them to:

> Sneak home and pray you'll never know
> The hell where youth and laughter go.

It was with poems like these that Sassoon, more than any other trench poet writing in English, brought home to an uninformed public the true reality of the ghastly nature of the war.

Although a number of A. A. Milne's whimsical war poems appeared in *Punch* during the war, the mordant sarcasm of "O.B.E." was deemed inappropriate and unacceptable for the magazine at that time. The poem had to wait until 1921 for publication.

The section "After the War" begins with Alex de Candole's desire to replace trenches, bombs and shells by the cattle and heather of the Wiltshire downs, in other words, another example of the struggle for supremacy between the anti-landscape of war and the pastoral landscape of peace.

In "Post Bellum" Geoffrey Fyson's portentously sonorous phrases and archaic diction project into a future when tourists will visit the front in order to "Traverse for holiday the hallow'd soil." He foresees there will be those who will even "envy us the life / Of changing scenes and perils manifold." Such people will inevitably distort the reality of that experience by "Casting a gloss of glory on our strife." He hopes that some proper memory of sacrifice for the sake of peace will survive and be remembered, however faintly and imperfectly.

In "A Farewell to Arms" Digby Haseler updates the uses for military equipment and arms referred to in the line he quotes from George Peele's sixteenth-century poem:

> My helmet now shall hang above my bed,
>   My pistol serve to scare birds from the grain,
> And even my gas-mask stand me in good stead
>   Whenever I clean out the farmyard drain.

In the extract from "To My Brother" Jeffery Day describes in convincing detail the landscape and wildlife of the Fens, an area that was well-known to him and one that he loved greatly (he was born at St. Ives, Huntingdonshire). He sees himself once more in this familiar landscape after the war. He says that while he moves through such a landscape either at dawn in winter or on a summer's night he will be aware of the closeness to him of his dead brother.

Greville Cooke's "Pin-Pricks" offers an unusual post-war civilian slant on the war. The poem records the rediscovery of the traces of markers on a former map of the war, kept by civilians at home, attempting to follow the fluctuating movements of the line as British troops advanced or retreated. The map and the flags have disappeared, just as, some ten or twelve years on, the trenches, shell-holes and craters have mostly been filled in and levelled. Only the pin-pricks in a banal image of an English village remain for children to wonder at. To the poet who charted these movements each of these tiny marks is the "token of a million high-held hearts," and represents painful memories for the relatives of the dead. We are used to condemnation by the fighting men of the role of newspapers' and their wartime propaganda. It is rare to find a civilian poet condemning the popular press of the day. He says that those who fought were "Snared by a Press gang" with their "paper patriotism." The fighting is presented for the most part in the form of generalized abstractions: "monotony," "murder," "stalemate." The closet approximation to the reality of war is "Stabbing steel." The effects of the war are "Insanity, loss of faith, bewilderment, despair, / Fear, agony of death and mutilation." This legacy follows the telling use of the pun, "No use, then, kicking against the pricks." The insertion of a pun in a solemn poem runs the risk of seriously undermining the poet's message, but in the present context it can be argued that Cooke's audacious use of such a risky device is justified.

Sassoon's "On Passing the New Menin Gate" is a late poem, and, like the previous poem by Cooke, and Sorley's youthful "The Tempest," falls outside the war years. He informs us that he began it in Brussels in July 1927 and finished it in London in January 1928 (Hart-Davis 153). The Menin Gate at Ypres is one of the most celebrated memorials of the Great War. It was designed by Sir Reginald Blomfield and inaugurated on 24 July 1927. The archway of the gate forms the British Memorial to the Missing and bears the names of nearly 55,000 men who died between 1914 and 15 August 1917 and who have no known grave.[29] Once again Sassoon finds the appropriately antiheroic tone and attitude with which the men commemorated in this way would surely have agreed. He is offended by the yawning gulf, the glaring polarization, between the vulgarity of this mammoth structure, which he dismisses as "a pile of peace-complacent stone," and "The unheroic Dead who fed the guns," "Those doomed, conscripted, unvictorious ones." This poem may be regarded as Sassoon's final disgusted and disenchanted word on the War he fought in and survived, although he did subsequently write three more minor war poems in 1933–34: "War Experience," "Ex-Service," and "Asking for it."

NOTES

1. Edward Davison (ed.), *Cambridge Poets 1914–1920. An Anthology.* Cambridge: Heffer & Sons Ltd., 1921.
2. Catherine Reilly, *English Poetry of the First World War: A Bibliography.* London: George Prior, 1978.
3. Anne Powell, *A Deep Cry.* Palladour Books, 1993.
4. Martin Taylor, *Lads: Love Poetry of the Trenches.* Constable, 1989.
5. John Silkin, *The Penguin Book of First World War Poetry.* Penguin, 1979.
6. Catherine Reilly, *Scars Upon my Heart. Women's Poetry and Verse of the First World War.* Virago, 1981. Also contained in her *The Virago Book of Women's War Poetry and Verse.* Virago, 1997.
7. G. V. Carey, *War List of the University of Cambridge, 1914–1918.* Cambridge University Press, 1921.
8. K. S. Inglis, " 'The Homecoming': The War Memorial Movement in Cambridge, England," *Journal of Contemporary History* 27 (1992): 583–605.
9. Samuel Hynes, *A War Imagined: The First World War and English Culture.* The Bodley Head, 1990, 109–19.
10. Rupert Hart-Davis, ed., *Siegfried Sassoon: The War Poems.* Faber & Faber, 1983, p. 15.
11. Bernard Bergonzi, *Heroes' Twilight.* Constable, 1965, p. 41.
12. John H. Johnston, *English Poetry of the First World War: A Study in the Evolution of Lyric and Narrative Form.* Princeton University Press, 1964, p. 30.
13. *Stand* 4, no. 3 (1960): 30–31.
14. Adrian Caesar, *Taking it Like a Man: Suffering, Sexuality and the War Poets: Brooke, Sassoon, Owen, Graves.* Manchester University Press, 1993, p. 53.
15. Jon Silkin, *Out of Battle: The Poetry of the Great War.* Oxford University Press, 1972; Routledge & Kegan Paul, 1987, p. ix.
16. Robert Rhodes James, *Gallipoli.* B. T. Batsford Ltd., 1965; Pan Books Ltd., 1974, pp. 333–36. John Masefield, *Gallipoli.* W. Heinemann Ltd, 1916, pp. 169–72.

17. Michael Copp, *From Emmanuel to the Somme: The War Writings of A. E. Tomlinson*. Cambridge: Lutterworth Press, 1997, p. 54.

18. Rupert Hart-Davis, ed., *Siegfried-Sassoon: War Diaries 1915–1918*. Faber & Faber, 1983, p. 148–49.

19. Jean Moorcroft Wilson, *Siegfried Sassoon: The Making of a War Poet, A Biography (1886–1918)*. Duckworth, 1998, p. 340.

20. Michael Thorpe, *Siegfried Sassoon: A Critical Study*. Oxford University Press, 1967, p. 34.

21. Jean Moorcroft Wilson, ed., *The Collected Poems of Charles Hamilton Sorley*. London: Cecil Woolf, 1985, p. 70.

22. Tim Cross, *The Lost Voices of World War I: An International Anthology of Writers, Poets and Playwrights*. London: Bloomsbury Publishing, 1988, p. 60.

23. *Times Literary Supplement*, 31 May 1917.

24. Patrick J. Quinn, *The Great War and the Missing Muse: The Early Writings of Robert Graves and Siegfried Sassoon*. Associated University Presses, 1994, p. 191.

25. Patrick Campbell, *Siegfried Sassoon: A Study of the War Poetry*. McFarland & Co., 1999, p. 191.

26. Rupert Hart-Davis, ed., *Siegfried Sassoon: The War Poems*. Faber & Faber, 1983, p. 49.

27. Sanford Sternlicht, *Siegfried Sassoon*. Twayne, 1993, p. 41.

28. Homer, *The Iliad,*, translated by W. H. D. Rouse. Edinburgh: Thomas Nelson & Sons Ltd., 1938, p. 246.

29. Rose E. B. Coombs, *Before Endeavours Fade: A Guide to the Battlefields of the First World War*. Battle of Britain Prints International Ltd., 1976, p. 29–30.

Premonition

The Tempest

The tempest is coming.
The sky is so dark,
The bee has stopped humming
And down flies the lark.

The clouds are all uttering
Strange words in the sky;
They are growling and muttering
As if they would die.

Some forked lightning passes
And lights up the sky;
A moment of glory
And then it will die.

The rain is beginning,
The sky is so dark,
The bird has stopped singing
And down flies the lark.

                    Charles Hamilton Sorley

Early Days

Two sonnets on the Declaration of War by Great Britain, on the 4th August, 1914

Casus Belli

When love of Country, rid of Faction's blight,
Deep drowns the clamour of fierce party cries,
Till all the nation stirred to high emprise,
With soul aflame, for Freedom's cause will fight,
Unchecked, shall despot flaunt his ruthless might,
And think, base traitor, tho' in friendly guise,
With bribes, Britannia's arm to paralyse,
While man, at Duty's call, will die for Right?
Much as we loathe thee, War, and thy fell train
Of woe untold, betrayal loathe we more,
Scorning to see the star of Honour wane:
Then with this thought let slumbering Faith awake,
E'en if our hosts must tread thy fields of gore,
When Right unsheathes the sword, will God forsake?

Ante Pacem Honor

Shall Britain's sword within the scabbard bide,
When Justice needs the sharpness of its blade,
And threatened allies seek its trusted aid,
To strike for Freedom by their gallant side?
Shall not that sword with foeman's blood be dyed,
To check mad despot in his pirate raid,
And, bared at Duty's call, face, unafraid,
The vengeance vowed by arrogance and pride?
Well man may shrink from Battle's ghastly sight,
And shudder at the thought of fiendish strife,
When love thro' blinding tears beholds its dead;
Yet better far brave death than sullied life,

And sullied his, who paths of Peace would tread,
When War alone can keep his honour bright.

Oswald Norman

Many Sisters to Many Brothers

When we fought campaigns (in the long Christmas rains)
    With soldiers spread in troops on the floor,
I shot as straight as you, my losses were as few,
    My victories as many, or more.
And when in naval battle, amid cannon's rattle,
    Fleet met fleet in the bath,
My cruisers were as trim, my battleships as grim,
    My submarines cut as swift a path.
Or, when it rained too long, and the strength of the strong
    Surged up and broke away with blows,
I was as fit and keen, my fists hit as clean,
    Your black eye matched my bleeding nose.
Was there a scrap or ploy in which you, the boy,
    Could better me? You could not climb higher,
Ride straighter, run as quick (and to smoke made you sick)
    . . . . But I sit here and you're under fire.

Oh, it's you that have the luck, out there in blood and muck:
    You were born beneath a kindly star;
All we dreamt, I and you, you can really go and do,
    And I can't, the way things are.
In a trench you are sitting, while I am knitting
    A hopeless sock that never gets done.
Well, here's luck, my dear;—and you've got it, no fear;
    But for me . . . . a war is poor fun.

Rose Macaulay

Dedication

To W. D. G., J. C. B., and other young soldiers

We have heard the bees and felt the sun grow hot on the face together,
    And watched the great clouds tumbling up across the Sussex down;
We found the same clouds farther north and the bees among the heather,
    Where the woods are old and silent and the pools are dark and brown.

We've read and laughed and played, good Lord! and talked the slow sun under,
    And heard the nightjars whirring and the rooks go home to bed,
And watched the harvest moon come up, a white and shining wonder,
    And all the bright star-companies go marching overhead.

The sweetest hour of all sweet hours is the hour when, long unbroken,
    A comfort and a silence fall that do not ask for speech;
The finest word of all fine words is the word that stays unspoken,
    But rests with both a crystal thought no utterance can reach.

God grant, dear lad, that once again we walk the moors together,
    And greet the sun and feel the wind blow fresh on face and lips,
Or stretch and dream upon the down in golden summer weather
    And watch our thoughts flock from us like the swift white wings of ships.

John L. C. Brown

From Whitechapel

A white and wolfish face, with fangs
    Half-snarling out of flaccid lips;
An unkempt head that loosely hangs;
    Shoulders that cower from gaoler's grips;

Eyes furtive in their greedy glance;
    Slim fingers not untaught to thieve;—
He shambles forward to the chance
    His whole life's squalor to retrieve.

                        John A. Nicklin

1814–1914

On reading The Dynasts

Read here the tale how England fought for freedom
Under Pitt and Castlereagh;
Gave unstintingly of her blood and treasure
To break a tyrant's sway.

'Europe in danger—her liberties imperilled.'
So the statesmen cried.
Stern, stupid Englishmen, foolishly believing them,
Marched and fought and died.

When the Corsican was broken and the pale suffering peoples
Thought their freedom due;
France got—her Bourbons back; Italy—her Bomba,
England—Peterloo.

A hundred years passed—once again:—'The liberties
Of Europe are at stake!'
Once again the statesmen bid the silent Englishmen
Die for freedom's sake.

Stern, stupid Englishmen, nowise disbelieving them,
March cheerfully away,

Heedless of the story of their fathers' 'War for Freedom'
Under Pitt and Castlereagh.

William N. Ewer

A Letter from Ealing Broadway Station

(From E.M.W.T.)

'Night. Fog. Tall through the murky gloom
The coloured lights of signals loom,
And underneath my boot I feel
The long recumbent lines of steel.
As up and down the beat I tramp
My face and hair are wet with damp;
My hands are cold—that's but a trifle—
And I must mind the sentry's rifle.
'Twould be a foolish way to die,
Mistaken for a German spy!
Hardest of all is just to keep
Open my eyelids drugged with sleep.

Stand back! With loud metallic crash
And lighted windows all a-flash
The train to Bristol past me booms.

I wonder who has got my rooms!
I like to think that Frank is there,
And Willie in the basket-chair,
While Ernest, with his guileless looks,
Is making havoc in my books.
The smoke-rings rise, and we discuss
Friendship, and What Life Means to Us,
What is it that the kitchens lack,
And where we'll take our tramp next vac.
Those girls at Newnham whom I taught
I'll spare them each a friendly thought . . .

An hour to dawn! I'd better keep
Moving, or I shall fall asleep.

75

I've had before my eyes these days
The fires of Antwerp all ablaze.
(The startled women scream and weep;
Only the dead have time to sleep.)
I'd like to feel that I was helping
To send those German curs a-yelping.
Well, if I serve the Belgian nation
By guarding Ealing Broadway station,
I'll guard it gladly, never fear.

Sister, good-night; the dawn is here.'

Cambridge, October 11, 1914

Aelfrida Tillyard

The Song of Sheffield

Shells, shells, shells!
   The song of the city of steel;
Hammer and turn and file,
    Furnace, and lathe, and wheel.
     Tireless machinery,
     Man's ingenuity,
Making a way for the martial devil's meal.

Shells, shells, shells,
   Out of the furnace's blaze;
Roll, roll, roll,
    Into the workshop's maze.
     Ruthless machinery
     Boring eternally
Boring a hole for the shattering charge that stays.

Shells, shells, shells!
   The song of the city of steel;
List to the devils' mirth,
    Hark to their laughter's peal:
     Sheffield's machinery
Crushing humanity
'Neath devil-ridden death's impassive heel.

Robert H. Beckh

The Old Soldiers

We come from dock and shipyard, we come from car and train,
We come from foreign countries to slope our arms again,
And, forming fours by numbers or turning to the right,
We're learning all our drill again and 'tis a pretty sight.

Our names are all unspoken, our regiments forgotten,
For some of us were pretty bad and some of us were rotten;
And some will misremember what once they learnt with pain
And hit a bloody sergeant and go to clink again.

Edward Shanks

Going in to Dinner

Beat the knife on the plate and the fork on the can,
For we're going in to dinner, so make all the noise you can,
Up and down the officer wanders, looking blue,
Sing a song to cheer him up, he wants his dinner too.
March into the village school, make the tables rattle
Like a dozen dam' machine-guns in the bloody battle,
Use your forks for drumsticks, use your plates for drums,
Make a most infernal clatter, here the dinner comes!

Edward Shanks

Drilling in Russell Square

The withered leaves that drift in Russell Square
Will turn to mud and dust and moulder there
And we shall moulder in the plains of France
Before these leaves have ceased from their last dance.
The hot sun triumphs through the fading trees,
The fading houses keep away the breeze
And the autumnal warmth strange dreams doth breed
As right and left the faltering columns lead.
'Squad, 'shun! Form fours . . . ' And once the France we knew
Was a warm distant place with sun shot through,
A happy land of gracious palaces,

And Paris! Paris! Where twice green the trees
Do twice salute the all delightful year!
(Though the sun lives, the trees are dying here.)
And Germany we thought a singing place,
Where in the hamlets dwelt a simple race,
Where th'untaught villager would still compose
Delicious things upon a girl or rose.
Well, all I suppose I shall see of France
Will be most clouded by an uhlan's lance,
Red fields from cover glimpsed be all I see
Of innocent, singing, peasant Germany.

'Form-four-rs! Form two deep!' We wheel and pair
And still the brown leaves drift in Russell Square.

Edward Shanks

Absolution

The anguish of the earth absolves our eyes
Till beauty shines in all that we can see.
War is our scourge; yet war has made us wise,
And, fighting for our freedom, we are free.

Horror of wounds and anger at the foe,
And loss of things desired; all these must pass.
We are the happy legion, for we know
Time's but a golden wind that shakes the grass.

There was an hour when we were loth to part
From life we longed to share no less than others.
Now, having claimed this heritage of heart,
What need we more, my comrades and my brothers?

Siegfried Sassoon

Officers' Mess

I

I search the room with all my mind,
Peering among those eyes;
For I am feverish to find
A brain with which my brain may talk,
Not that I think myself too wise,
But that I'm lonely, and I walk
Round the large place and wonder—No:
There's nobody, I fear,
Lonely as I, and here.

How they hate me. I'm a fool.
I can't play Bridge; I'm bad at Pool;
I cannot drone a comic song;
I can't talk Shop; I can't use Slang;
My jokes are bad, my stories long;
My voice will falter, break or hang,
Not blurt the sour sarcastic word,
And so my swearing sounds absurd.

II

But came the talk: I found
Three or four others for an argument.
I forced their pace. They shifted their dull ground,
And went
Sprawling about the passages of Thought.
We tugged each other's words until they tore.
They asked me my philosophy: I brought
Bits of it forth and laid them on the floor.
They laughed, and so I kicked the bits about,
Then put them in my pocket one by one,
I, sorry I had brought them out,
They, grateful for the fun.

And when these words had thus been sent
Jerking about, like beetles round a wall,
Then one by one to dismal sleep we went:
There was no happiness at all
In that short hopeless argument

Through yawns and on the way to bed
Among men waiting to be dead.

Harold Monro

1914

I Peace

Now, God be thanked Who has matched us with this hour,
 And caught our youth, and wakened us from sleeping,
With hand made sure, clear eye, and sharpened power,
 To turn, as swimmers into cleanness leaping,
Glad from a world grown old and cold and weary,
 Leave the sick hearts that honour could not move,
And half-men, and their dirty songs and dreary,
 And all the little emptiness of love!

Oh! we, we have known shame, we have found release there,
 Where there's no ill, no grief, but sleep has mending,
  Naught broken save this body, lost but breath;
Nothing to shake the laughing heart's long peace there
 But only agony, and that has ending;
  And the worst friend and enemy is but Death.

II Safety

Dear! of all happy in the hour, most blest
 He who has found our hid security,
Assured in the dark tides of the world at rest,
 And heard our word, 'Who is so safe as we?'
We have found safety with all things undying,
 The winds, and morning, tears of men and mirth,
The deep night, and birds singing, and clouds flying,
 And sleep, and freedom, and the autumnal earth.
We have built a house that is not for Time's throwing.
 We have gained a peace unshaken by pain for ever.
War knows no power. Safe shall be my going,
 Secretly armed against all death's endeavour;
Safe though all safety's lost; safe where men fall;
And if these poor limbs die, safest of all.

III The Dead

Blow out, you bugles, over the rich Dead!
   There's none of these so lonely and poor of old,
   But dying, has made us rarer gifts than gold.
These laid the world away; poured out the red
Sweet wine of youth; gave up the years to be
   Of work and joy, and that unhoped serene,
   That men call age; and those who would have been
Their sons, they gave, their immortality.

Blow, bugles, blow! They brought us, for our dearth,
   Holiness, lacked so long, and Love, and Pain.
Honour has come back, as a king, to earth,
   And paid his subjects with a royal wage;
And Nobleness walks in our ways again;
   And we have come into our heritage.

IV The Dead

These hearts were woven of human joys and cares,
   Washed marvellously with sorrow, swift to mirth,
The years had given them kindness. Dawn was theirs,
   And sunset, and the colours of the earth.
These had seen movement, and heard music; known
   Slumber and waking; loved; gone proudly friended;
Felt the quick stir of wonder; sat alone;
   Touched flowers and furs and cheeks. All this is ended.

There are waters blown by changing winds to laughter
And lit by the rich skies, all day. And after,
   Frost, with a gesture, stays the waves that dance
And wandering loveliness. He leaves a white
   Unbroken glory, a gathered radiance,
A width, a shining peace, under the night.

V The Soldier

If I should die, think only this of me:
   That there's some corner of a foreign field
That is for ever England. There shall be
   In that rich earth a richer dust concealed;

81

A dust whom England bore, shaped, made aware,
  Gave once, her flowers to love, her ways to roam.
A body of England's, breathing English air,
  Washed by the rivers, blest by the suns of home.

And think, this heart, all evil shed away,
  A pulse in the eternal mind, no less
    Gives somewhere back the thoughts by England given;
Her sights and sounds; dreams happy as her day;
  And laughter, learnt of friends; and gentleness,
    In hearts at peace, under an English heaven.

Rupert Brooke

Over There

Picnic

July 1917

We lay and ate sweet hurt-berries
   In the bracken of Hurt Wood.
Like a quire of singers singing low
   The dark pines of the wood.

Behind us climbed the Surrey hills,
   Wild, wild in greenery;
At our feet the downs of Surrey broke
   To an unseen sea.

And life was bound in a still ring,
   Drowsy and quiet, and sweet . . .
When heavily up the south-east wind
   The great guns beat.

We did not wince, we did not weep,
   We did not curse or pray;
We drowsily heard, and someone said,
   'They sound clear today'.

We did not shake with pity and pain,
   Or sicken and blanch white.
We said, 'If the wind's from over there
   There'll be rain tonight'.

.   .   .

Once pity we knew, and rage we knew,
   And pain we knew, too well,
As we stared and peered dizzily
   Through the gates of hell.
But now hell's gates are an old tale;
   Remote the anguish seems;

The guns are muffled and far away,
    Dreams within dreams.

And far and far are Flanders mud,
    And the pain of Picardy;
And the blood that runs there runs beyond
    The wide waste sea.

We are shut about by guarding walls:
    (We have built them lest we run
Mad from dreaming of naked fear
    And of black things done).

We are ringed all round by guarding walls,
    So high they shut the view.
Not all the guns that shatter the world
    Can quite break through.

.   .   .

Oh, guns of France, oh, guns of France,
    Be still, you crash in vain . . .
Heavily up the south wind throb
    Dull dreams of pain, . . .

Be still, be still, south wind, lest your
    Blowing should bring the rain . . .
We'll lie very quiet on Hurt Hill,
    And sleep once again.

Oh, we'll lie quite still, nor listen nor look,
    While earth's bounds reel and shake,
Lest, battered too long, our walls and we
    Should break . . . should break . . .

                                    Rose Macaulay

The Farmer

I see a farmer walking by himself
In the ploughed field, returning like the day
To his dark nest. The plovers circle round
In the gray sky; the blackbird calls; the thrush
Still sings—but all the rest have gone to sleep.
I see the farmer coming up the field,
Where the new corn is sown, but not yet sprung;
He seems to be the only man alive
And thinking through the twilight of this world.
I know that there is war beyond those hills,
And I surmise, but cannot see the dead,
And cannot see the living in their midst—
So awfully and madly knit with death.
I cannot feel, but know that there is war,
And has been now for three eternal years,
Beyond the subtle cinctures of those hills.
I see the farmer coming up the field,
And as I look, imagination lifts
The sullen veil of alternating cloud,
And I am stunned by what I see behind
His solemn and uncompromising form:
Wide hosts of men who once could walk like him
In freedom, quite alone with night and day,
Uncounted shapes of living flesh and bone,
Worn dull, quenched dry, gone blind and sick, with war;
And they are him and he is one of them;
They see him as he travels up the field.
O God, how lonely freedom seems today!
O single farmer walking through the world,
They bless the seed in you that earth shall reap,
When they, their countless lives, and all their thoughts,
Lie scattered by the storm: when peace shall come
With stillness, and long shivers, after death.

Fredegond Shove

The Stones of Belgium

The Fort

Hear me. I was a fortress once—and now a grave.
Silenced, the guns and men beneath my ruin lie.
They spoke, and there was neither man nor God to save.
The very stones aloud for vengeance cry.

A Gravestone

I am a gravestone cross. Last spring a young wife died.
Deep down she sleeps, her baby by her side.
I stretch my cold grey arms to guard her rest.
Her husband marched away, and—God knows best.

Some Blackened Walls

Does He know best? The lone winds roam
Through shattered casements open to the sky.
I was a warm well-tended cottage home—
A wreckage left, when tides of war swept by.

A Brothel

Sin is eternal—sin and lust and pain—
And men shall haste to build my walls again.
I laughed to see the lads with Hatred make carouse,
For vaunted Peace is but a prim child-ridden spouse.

A Milestone

Five hundred years I stood. Along the endless roads
I watched the men go by, deep-burdened with their loads.
And some were wise and some were fools,
And all have lived in vain.
For those who trod the ways of Peace
By Time at last were slain.

The Fort

The dew of death is on the earth's wide brow.
Daylight is fled. We are all gravestones now.

The Earth

Have ye no faith? These winds and lashing rain,
Fire, darkness, and the white dawn's drenching dew
Shall make you pure for happiness anew.
Lie still, O stone, YE SHALL ARISE AGAIN.

(Cambridge, March 13, 1915)

Aelfrida Tillyard

The Three Crosses

The day dawned bleak and grey, and weary eyes
Opening from fitful sleep looked out once more
Upon the field of woe. The patient earth
Lay fouled with blood and riven with ruinous shard.
But while men slept the piteous husbandry
Of death was garnered in: one stricken son
Alone the mighty mother bore upon her breast,
Sole gleanings of that midnight harvesting.
    Derelict 'twixt friend and foe he agonised.
In the dim dawn alone. . . .

With the new day the battle raged anew,
And still his silence pleaded to the skies.
But Heaven seemed dumb, and all the swooning world
Was yielded to the sovranty of hate,
And wrath and pride and carnage stalked abroad.
Then God on high spoke gloriously: a form
Loomed sudden on our vision gaunt and grey,
Strode from the trenches, faced the fires of hell
And raised the wounded foeman tenderly.
We in amaze ceased fire, and stood aghast
As that gaunt figure staggered on and on,
Torn with a hail of bullets, to the edge
Of German trenches: very tenderly
The strong man laid his grievous burden there.
Then, as he staggered back, a thing befell
That in a moment dimmed each eye with tears,
And thunderous cheering broke from every throat.

Love kindles love, and deeds of bravery
Beget a noble emulation: quick as thought
Answers to thought, or echo follows voice
In some lone valley on a mountain side,
That deed of ruth bore fruitage: with a bound
A German—flower of all his nation's chivalry—
Tore from his breast the hard-won Iron Cross
And trembling pinned it o'er the noble heart.
A great silence fell: and then the opposed ranks
Sent forth a mighty cheer, and wrath lay dead
For one brief respite: and our hearts aflame
Thanked God that love is mightier still than hate,
That bravery makes one kindred of the world.
Then with a proud salute our hero turned
And, reeling as he came, was in our midst . . .

All day the battle raged, till pitiful night
Came on, and we were free to think again,
Again to glory in the glamour of that scene,
And all men swore that next the Iron Cross
That other should be pinned, most coveted
Of all rewards. But the great heart lay still;
And when the morrow broke, a cross of wood
Alone remained to tell men where he lay.

*   *   *

Was any love like his? The frozen South
Is glamorous with the imperishable name
Of him who died to save his friends from death,
That very gallant gentleman. But he
Our friend had died that one unknown,
Son of a race relentless as the grave,
Might live: was any other love like his?

"Forgive them for they know not what they do":
Down the long vista of the ages rings
That parent cry of every deed of love,
And from the Cross Divine Compassion spreads,
Kindling response, till earth's remotest shore
Rejoices in the tale, and He the Lord
Rejoices in the travail of His soul.

Strong Son of God, great Captain of the Brave!
Heroic souls to-day are knit with Thine,
And strongest manhood still acclaims Thy Cross:
To Thee we yield the glory of that deed;
For still Thy interception nerves the world,
And heroes are the offspring of Thy Blood.

Kenneth Saunders
(Christmastide, 1914)

Brothers

"Ut Omnes Unum Sint."

A True Incident

Is it for naught the immemorial pain,
The age-long yearning of the Heart of God
Crying, "Turn, My Sons, be reconciled,
And learn of Me the meek and lowly heart"?
The nations reel and stagger to their doom;
The war-lords muster their far-flung array,
And all the weary world incarnadine.
Is it in vain, ye warring sons of God,
That aeons travailled for your heritage?
Is it for nought the Cross, the Life laid down,
The Risen Glory of the Lord of Life?
Shall God be mocked, and Satan Lord of Hosts?
Is Jesus throned on high so impotent?

*   *   *

I pondered thus, and gazed upon the slain
Piled heap on heap in agony: a hand
Stretched here to heaven; there an upturned face
That dumbly pled to dumb and lowering skies.
And as I gazed, and sickened at the sight
Of carnage, Hell let loose, high carnival
Of Death, I saw a Jew, a Rabbi sable-clad,
Pondering the wreckage of fair human forms,

The shattered Temples of his God: amazed
He seemed to commune with the Nameless One.

*   *   *

From him my thoughts turned back to Calvary,
The drooping Head, the bursting Patriot Heart
That yearned with pity for His blinded race.
That broke for men who wrought the deed of shame.
"My God, My God", rang out the derelict cry,
But louder rang the cry of faith and hope,
And louder still the cry of love, "Forgive!
Forgive them, for they know not what they do."
And in the dawn a wail, I thought, arose
Of many voices, tortured men and maids,
Pleading the wrongs of all their ancient race,
Wrongs wrought by men who bore the Name of Christ.

*   *   *

But here a Frenchman in his agony
Raised piteous eyes and saw that priestly form:
"The Crucifix", he sobbed. "Lord Jesus, pity me!
That I may kiss the Prince of Peace and die."
Swift came the answer as the man of God
Stooped, and divine compassion kindling him,
Raised up a rugged Cross that marked a grave,
And held it meekly to the dying lips.
Then as he bent came the swift messenger
Of Death and struck him down. Together there
Christian and Jew lay dead on either side
The Cross that made them one. Ah! not in vain
That act of matchless love: Thy Cross, O Christ,
Stretching its arms to the four winds of Heaven,
Is still our promise of a far-off Peace,
Is still the token of Thy victory.
So Slav and Teuton, Jew and anti-Jew
Shall break their bonds of hatred and be one:
So comes Thy kingdom, Prince of Peace, indeed.

*   *   *

And what of him, who, dying, lived so well,
And sought to bring a brother's soul to peace?

Far-off methought a voice of majesty
Cried calm and kingly to his dying ears:
"Come, blessed of my Father, come at last!
To-day My brother in God's paradise
Thou, too, shalt kiss the Prince of Peace and live."

Kenneth Saunders
(Eastertide, 1915)

I Saw Them Laughing Once

I saw them laughing once; they held their sides
And laughed till old Olympus shook again,—
The blessed gods, who watch whate'er betides
On earth below, saw man with man in vain
Strive in besotted hate, crawl out at night
And creep about, and hide in fear the day,
Burrowing beneath the earth at dawn's first light,
And sleeping all the golden hours away
Of sun and pleasure; then when night grows chill,
Though bright the full moon shines upon the earth
He calls it dark, comes out, and works his will.
Small wonder surely for Olympus mirth,
At war, sans right, sans reason, and sans mind,
This wild supremest folly of mankind!

Alex C.V. de Candole

In That Rough Barn We Knelt

In that rough barn we knelt, and took and ate
Simply together there the bread divine,
The body of God made flesh, and drank in wine
His blood who died, to man self-dedicate.
And even while we knelt, a sound of hate
Burst sudden on us, as our shrieking line
Of guns flashed bursting death, a thunderous sign
Of raging evil in our human state.
Strange state! when good must use (nor other can)

93

The tools of ill, itself from ill to free,
And Christ must fight with Satan's armoury.
What strange and piteous contrast may we scan,
The shell that slays, and Christ upon the tree,
The love that died, and man that murders man!

Alec C.V. de Candole

August 1918
(In a French village)

I hear the tinkling of a cattle bell,
In the broad stillness of the afternoon;
High in the cloudless haze the harvest moon
Is pallid as the phantom of a shell.

A girl is drawing water from a well,
I hear the clatter of her wooden shoon;
Two mothers to their sleeping babies croon,
And the hot village feels the drowsy spell.

Sleep, child, the Angel of Death his wings has spread;
His engines scour the land, the sea, the sky;
And all the weapons of Hell's armoury

Are ready for the blood that is their bread;
And many a thousand men to-night must die,
So many that they will not count the dead.

Maurice Baring

A Vision

In paradise I lie of leaves and flowers:
Long boughs hang from above in luminous showers:
    Rose-scented the warm air.
A hidden water mingles its lisping sound
With the sultry music of bees, and the sense is drowned
In a pool of warm delight. But as it drowses
Deep and to outward things serenely closes,

Some freak of the uncharted mind lays bare . . .
No richer summer, deeper-hearted roses,
But greyness, rain, and ruin, and in the air
A flying sorrow as some forlorn shell whines
From silence into silence over the still
Brown deserts of torn earth, and the charred stains
Of shell-bursts, and the scrawled unending lines
Of battered trench where, blackening in the rains,
The dead lie out upon the naked hill.

Martin Armstrong

Going up the Line

O consolation and refreshment breathed
From the young Spring with apple-blossom wreathed,
    Whose certain coming blesses
All life with token of immortality.
And from the ripe beauty and human tenderness
And reconcilement and tranquillity
Which are the spirit of all things grown old.
    For now that I have seen
The curd-white hawthorn once again
    Break out on the new green,
And through the iron gates in the long blank wall
    Have viewed across a screen
Of rosy apple-blossom the grey spire
And low red roofs and humble chimney-stacks,
And stood in spacious courtyards of old farms,
And heard green virgin wheat sing to the breeze,
And the drone of ancient worship rise and fall
In the dark church, and talked with simple folk
Of farm and village, dwelling near the earth,
Among earth's ancient elemental things:
    I can with heart made bold
Go back into the ways of ruin and death
With step unflagging and with quiet breath,
For drawn from the hidden Spirit's deepest well
I carry in my soul a power to quell
    All ills and terrors such as these can hold.

Martin Armstrong

Last Song

All my songs are risen and fled away;
  (Only the brave birds stay);
All my beautiful songs are broken or fled.
  My poor songs could not stay
Among the filth and the weariness and the dead.

There was bloody grime on their light, white feathery wings,
  (Hear how that lark still sings),
And their eyes were the eyes of dead men that I knew.
  Only a madman sings
When half of his friends lie asleep for the rain and the dew.

The flowers will grow over the bones of my friends;
  (The birds' song never ends);
Winter and summer, their fair flesh turns to clay.
  Perhaps before all ends
My songs will come again that have fled away.

Henry L. Simpson

Here Dead Lie We

Here dead lie we because we did not choose
  To live and shame the land from which we sprung.
Life, to be sure, is nothing much to lose;
  But young men think it is, and we were young.

A. E. Housman

Harrow and Flanders

Here in the marshland, past the battered bridge,
  One of a hundred grains untimely sown,
Here, with his comrades of the hard-won ridge,
  He rests, unknown.

His horoscope had seemed so plainly drawn -
  School triumphs earned apace in work and play;

Friendships at will; then love's delightful dawn
  And mellowing day;

Home fostering hope; some service to the State;
  Benignant age; then the long tryst to keep
Where in the yew-tree shadow congregate
  His fathers sleep.

Was here the one thing needful to distil
  From life's alembic, through this holier fate,
The man's essential soul, the hero will?
  We ask; and wait.

Lord Crewe

The Soldier's Cigarette

(October 1915)

I'm cheap and insignificant,
  I'm easy quite to get,
In every place I show my face
  They call me cigarette.

They buy me four a penny, throw
  Me down without regret,
The elegant, the nonchalant,
  The blasé cigarette.

I'm small and nothing much to see,
  But men won't soon forget
How unafraid my part I've played,
  The dauntless cigarette.

When trenches are all water-logged
  I'm thereabouts, you bet,
With cheery smile the hours I while,
  The patient cigarette.

I sit within the trenches and
  Upon the parapet;

Jack Johnson's shock with scorn I mock,
  The careless cigarette.

If bullets whiz and Bill gets hit,
  Don't hurry for the 'vet.',
It's 'I'm alright, give us a light.'
  And 'Where's my cigarette?'

Ubiquitous and agile too,
  I'm but a youngster yet,
The debonair, the savoir faire
  Abandoned cigarette.

When meals are few and far between,
  When spirit's ebb has set,
When comrades fall, and death's gates call,
  Who's there but cigarette?

I cool the mind and quiet the brain
  When danger's to be met;
When more is vain I ease the pain,
  Immortal cigarette!

Robert H. Beckh

Gold Braid

Same old crossing, same old boat.
  Same old dust round Rouen way.
Same old narsty one-franc note,
  Same old 'Mercy, sivvoo play',
Same old scramble up the line,
  Same old 'orse-box, same old stror,
Same old weather, wet or fine,
  Same old blooming War.
    Ho Lor, it isn't a dream,
      It's just as it used to be, every bit;
    Same old whistle and same old bang,
      And me to stay 'ere till I'm 'it.

*

'Twas up by Loos I got me first;
  I just dropped gently, crawled a yard
And rested sickish with a thirst—
  The 'eat, I thought, and smoking 'ard . . .
Then someone offers me a drink,
  What poets call 'the cooling draft',
And seeing 'im I done a think:
  'Blighty', I thinks—and laughed.

I'm not a soldier natural,
  No more than most of us to-day;
I run a business with a pal
  (Meaning the Missis) Fulham way;
Greengrocery—the cabbages
  And fruit and things I take myself,
And she has daffs and crocuses
  A-smiling on a shelf.

'Blighty', I thinks. The doctor knows;
  'E talks of punctured damn-the-things.
It's me for Blighty. Down I goes;
  I ain't a singer, but I sings;
'Oh, 'oo goes 'ome?' I sort of 'ums;
  'Oh, 'oo's for dear old England's shores?'
And by-and-by Southampton comes—
  'Blighty!' I says and roars.

I s'pose I thought I done my bit;
  I s'pose I thort the War would stop;
I saw myself a-getting fit
  With Missis at the little shop;
The same like as it used to be,
  The same old markets, same old crowd,
The same old marrers, same old me,
  But 'er as proud as proud . . .

        *

The regiment is where it was,
  I'm in the same old ninth platoon;
New faces most, and keen becos
  They 'ope the thing is ending soon;
I ain't complaining, mind, but still,

99

When later on some newish bloke
Stops one and laughs, 'A Blighty, Bill',
I'll wonder, 'Where's the joke?'

Same old trenches, same old view,
   Same old rats and just as tame,
Same old dug-outs, nothing new,
   Same old smell, the very same,
Same old bodies out in front,
   Same old strafe from 2 till 4,
Same old scratching, same old 'unt,
   Same old bloody War.

   Ho Lor, it isn't a dream,
      It's just as it used to be, every bit;
   Same old whistle and same old bang
   And me out again to be 'it.

                              A. A. Milne

War Meditations

When the snow lies crisp and sparkling o'er the frozen sea of
   mud
Which lies round Combles and Péronne;
When your veins are full of icicles instead of warm red blood,
And your circulation's absolutely gone;
When your fingers get so numb your glasses won't stay near
   your eyes,
And you're tired of watching movement in Bapaume,
Don't you really sometimes feel you'd like to have a damned
   good cry,
When your thoughts begin to turn towards your home.
When your D111's out of order and the dug-out's cold and
   damp,
And your best telephonists are sick with 'flu,
When you find that you've forgotten on which point you were
   to clamp,
And you know you have to register at two.
When the watch that you have synchronised an hour ago has
   stopped,

And the Major wants the F.O.O.'s report,
When you haven't got the faintest notion where the first
   round dropped,
And the infantry report rounds falling short.

When you're passing Ginchy corner and the Hun begins to
   strafe,
And you want to throw yourself down in the mud,
But you daren't because you know that the telephonists
   would laugh,
So you can but hope the next will be a dud,
When you get to your O.P. and you find you've worked your
   factors wrong,
And you're well within the hundred per cent zone,
Have you never felt that feeling when your whole soul seems
   to long
For a home, a dog, a wife to call your own.

Vivian T. Pemberton

The Song of a Sad Siege Gunner
(Dedicated to all kindred disillusioned souls that have once
believed in Journalists and Schools of Gunnery)

I used to think I'd like to see the thing that men call war,
To hear machine-gun bullets swish and high explosives roar,
To feel my blood course through my veins afire with battle's
   lust,
I used to think I'd sell my soul for one good bayonet thrust.

Beach Thomas filled my brains with many dreams of fierce
   delight,
Of trenches full of sturdy Britons spoiling for a fight,
Of grey dawn rising slowly o'er the valley of the Somme,
Of great clouds rent asunder by the bursts of shell and bomb.

I.G's who did a Cook's tour once a year to G.H.Q.
With formulae and slide rules slightly changed my point of
   view,
They filled my brain with factors and siege gunners' rules of
   thumb,
But still I lived in hopes of mighty fights that were to come.

101

I read the rules of ranging till I knew them off by heart,
I studied tracts on camouflage and trajectory charts,
I had the M.V.'s painted on the muzzles of the guns,
And dreamed each night I'd bracketed advancing mobs of Huns.

At railhead where we spent three days the B.S.M. went sick,
I almost wept for him, poor chap, it seemed a bit too thick,
And when with breaking voice I said good-bye, the brave man
    wore
Upon his face a patient smile—he had been out before.

Then we went up the line. I'll not forget my first abode,
A little rat-infested German dug-out near a road.
'Aha, at last', I thought, 'discomfort! Soon we'll see a fight.'
And of the mighty deeds I'd do next day I dreamt all night.

For three long months we stayed there in that dreary sea of
    mud,
Surrounded by remains of what had once been flesh and blood.
We made a mighty dug-out thirty feet down in the earth
And there to many strange new thoughts my nimble mind gave
    birth.

I thought of all the brass hats and the tabs, red, green, and blue,
That make so picturesque the colour scheme at G.H.Q.
And mentally I ceased to stoop to kiss their garments' hem,
I even dared one day to greet a passing A.P.M.

One dud day when the mist was thick and snipers couldn't
    snipe,
Or gunners range, I sat in my O.P. and smoked my pipe,
And listened to the duck-boards creak for an hour and a half
Beneath the martial tread of half the British General Staff.

I was battery F.O.O. for eight months and a day.
How many rounds I have observed I should not like to say,
But I've never used a slide rule or any formulae
And I do not even know the melting point of N.C.T.

The Gym beneath whose baleful yoke at Lydd I bowed my head
Was buried deep and o'er its grave a grateful prayer I said.
We wrote it off destroyed by shell-fire, thus we hid our sin,
And saved instead two dozen Vermouth and a case of gin.

I've heard the anguished stricken cry of strong men and of
   weak,
I've seen the limbless try to walk, the jawless try to speak,
I've seen brave men grow sick with fear and grovel in the dust,
But never have I seen blood drawn with one good Bayonet
   thrust.

Vivian T. Pemberton

Mine-Sweeping Trawlers

Not ours the fighter's glow,
   The glory, and the praise.
Unnoticed to and fro
   We pass our dangerous ways.
We sift the drifting sea,
   And blindly grope beneath;
Obscure and toilsome we,
   The fishermen of death.

But when the great ships go
   To battle through the gloom,
Our hearts beat high to know
   We cleared their path of doom.

Edward H. Young

North Sea

Dawn on the drab North Sea!—
Colourless, cold, and depressing,
With the sun that we long to see
Refraining from its blessing.
To the westward—sombre as doom:
To the eastward—grey and foreboding:
Comes a slow, vibrating boom—
The sound of a mine exploding.

Day on the drear North Sea!—
Wearisome, drab, and relentless.

103

The low clouds swiftly flee;
Bitter the sky, and relentless.
Nothing at all in sight
Save the mast of a sunken trawler,
Fighting her long, last fight
With the waves that mouth and maul her.

Gale on the bleak North Sea!—
Howling a dirge in the rigging.
Slowly and toilfully
Through the great, grey breakers digging,
Thus we make our way,
Hungry, and wet, and weary,
Soaked with the sleet and the spray,
Desolate, damp, and dreary.

Fog in the dank North Sea!—
Silent and clammily dripping.
Slowly and mournfully,
Ghostlike, goes the shipping.
Sudden across the swell
Come the fog-horns hoarsely blaring
Or the clank of a warning bell,
To leave us vainly staring.

Night on the black North Sea!—
Black as hell's darkest hollow.
Peering anxiously,
We search for the ships that follow.
One are the sea and the sky,
Dim are the figures near us,
With only the sea-bird's cry
And the swish of the waves to cheer us.

Death on the wild North Sea!—
Death from the shell that shatters
(Death we will face with glee,
'Tis the weary wait that matters):—
Death from the guns that roar,
And the splinters weirdly shrieking.
'Tis a fight to the death; 'tis war;
And the North Sea is redly reeking!

Jeffery Day

On the Wings of the Morning

A sudden roar, a mighty rushing sound,
  A jolt or two, a smoothly sliding rise,
A tumbled blur of disappearing ground,
  And then all sense of motion slowly dies.
    Quiet and calm, the earth slips past below,
    As underneath a bridge still waters flow.

My turning wing inclines towards the ground;
  The ground itself glides up with graceful swing
And at the plane's far tip twirled slowly round,
  And then drops from sight again beneath the wing
    To slip away serenely as before,
    A cubist-patterned carpet on the floor.

Hills gently sink and valleys gently fill.
  The flattened fields grow ludicrously small;
Slowly they pass beneath and slower still
  Until they hardly seem to move at all.
    Then suddenly they disappear from sight,
    Hidden by fleeting wisps of faded white.

The wing-tips, faint and dripping, dimly show,
  Blurred by the wreaths of mist that intervene.
Weird, half-seen shadows flicker to and fro
  Across the pallid fog-bank's blinding screen.
    At last the choking mists release their hold,
    And all the world is silver, blue, and gold.

The air is clear, more clear than sparkling wine;
  Compared with this, wine is a turgid brew.
The far horizon makes a clean-cut line
  Between the silver and the depthless blue.
    Out of the snow-white level reared on high
    Glittering hills surge up to meet the sky.

Outside the windscreen's shelter gales may race:
  But in the seat a cool and gentle breeze
Blows steadily upon my grateful face.
    As I sit motionless and at my ease,
    Contented just to loiter in the sun
    And gaze around me till the day is done.

And so I sit, half sleeping, half awake,
   Dreaming a happy dream of golden days,
Until at last, with a reluctant shake
   I rouse myself, and with a lingering gaze
     At all the splendour of the shining plain
     Make ready to come down again.

The engine stops: a pleasant silence reigns—
   Silence, not broken, but intensified
By the soft, sleepy wires' insistent strains,
   That rise and fall, as with a sweeping glide
     I slither down the well-oiled sides of space,
     Towards a lower, less enchanted place.

The clouds draw nearer, changing as they come.
   Now like a flash, fog grips me by the throat.
Down goes the nose: at once the wires' low hum
   Begins to rise in volume and in note,
     Till, as I hurtle from the choking cloud
     It swells into a scream, high-pitched, and loud.

The scattered hues and shades of green and brown
   Fashion themselves into the land I know,
Turning and twisting, as I spiral down
   Towards the landing-ground; till, skimming low,
     I glide with slackening speed across the ground,
     And come to rest with lightly grating sound.

                     Jeffery Day

The Call of the Air

Have you ever sat in crystal space, enjoying the sensations
   Of an eagle hovered high above the earth,
Gazing down on man's ridiculous and infantile creations
   And judging them according to their worth?
Have you looked upon a basin small enough to wash your face
in,
   With a few toy-ships collected by the shore,
And then realised with wonder that if those toys go under
   Nine-tenths of Britain's navy is no more?

Have you seen a khaki maggot crawling down a thread of
cotton—
    The route march of a regiment or so?
Have you seen the narrow riband, unimportant, half-forgotten,
    That tells you that the Thames is far below?
Have you glanced with smiling pity at the world's most famous
city,
    A large grey smudge that barely strikes the eye?
Would you like to see things truly and appreciate them duly?
    Well then do it, damn you, do it; learn to fly!

Have you left the ground in murkiness, all clammy, grey, and
soaking,
    And struggled through the dripping, dirty white?
Have you seen the blank sides closing in and felt that you were
choking,
    And then leapt into a land of blazing light,
Where the burnished sun is shining on the cloud's bright silver
lining,
    A land where none but fairy feet have trod,
Where the splendour nearly blinds you and the wonder of it
binds you,
    And you know you are in heaven, close to God?

Have you tumbled from the sky until your wires were shrilly
screaming,
    And watched the earth go spinning round about?
Have you felt the hard air beat your face until your eyes were
streaming?
    Have you turned the solar system inside out?
Have you seen earth rush to meet you and the fields spread out
to greet you,
    And flung them back to have another try?
Would it fill you with elation to be boss of all creation?
    Well then do it, damn you, do it; learn to fly!

Have you fought a dummy battle, diving, twisting, pirouetting,
    At a lightning speed that takes away your breath?
Have you been so wildly thrilled that you have found yourself
forgetting
    That it's practice, not a battle to the death?
Have you hurtled low through narrow, tree-girt spaces like an
arrow—

Seen things grow and disappear like pricked balloons?
Would you feel the breathless joy of it and hear the thrilling
noise of it,
    The swish, the roar, the ever-changing tunes?
Have you chased a golden sunbeam down a gold and silver
alley,
    With pink and orange jewels on the floor?
Have you raced a baby rainbow round a blue and silver valley,
    Where purple caves throw back the engine's roar?
Have you seen the lights that smoulder on a cloud's resplendent
shoulder
    Standing out before a saffron-coloured sky?
Would you be in splendid places and illimitable spaces?
    Well then do it, damn you, do it; learn to fly!

Jeffery Day

Dawn

'Machines will raid at dawn', they say:
It's always dawn, or just before;
Why choose this wretched time of day
    For making war?

From all the hours of light there are
Why do they always choose the first?
Is it because they know it's far
    And far the worst?

Is it a morbid sense of fun
That makes them send us day by day
A target for the sportive Hun?—
    Who knows our way,

And waits for us at dawn's first peep,
Knowing full well we shall be there,
And he, when that is done, may sleep
    Without a care.

And was it not Napoleon
Who said (in French) these words, 'Lor' lumme!

No man can hope to fight upon
   An empty tummy'?

Yet every morn we bold bird-boys
Clamber into our little buses,
And go and make a futile noise
   With bombs and cusses.

And every night the orders tell
The same monotonous old story,
'Machines will raid at dawn.' To hell
   With death or glory!

Why can't they let us lie in bed
And, after breakfast and a wash,
Despatch us, clean and fully fed,
   To kill the Boche?

I hate the dawn, as dogs hate soap:
And on my heart, when I am done,
You'll find the words engraved, 'Dawn hope-
Less, streak of, one.'

Jeffery Day

Suvla Bay

October 1915

In silhouettes of silver and gray,
With tall fantastic peaks against the sky
Of crimson and saffron in the dying day,
Imbros and Samothrace to westward lie.
No seabirds homing to the salt lake fly
Across the sapphire waters of the bay,
But thunder-echoes roll and faint and die
As the lean war-ship seeks her distant prey.
Yet not to westward in the sunset's fire
Our eyes are set, tho' there a splendour burns.
Nay—eastward—where the morning light comes in—
The grave of hope—the death-place of desire—

The goal to which each ardent spirit still yearns,
The sombre-circled heights we could not win.

                                    Frederic W. D. Bendall

The Blizzard

Suvla, November 27, 1915

The night was dark as hell-mouth, the wind was bitter cold,
And there was little comfort in a sodden blanket rolled.
A foot or more of water, an inch or two of mud
Was what we had to walk in before came down—the flood.
It caught the shivering sentries along the parapet,
The front trench was abrim before they knew that they were
    wet,
Full seven feet deep the trenches were, the men were weighted
    down
With kit and ammunition, and mostly had to drown.
Behind was soon no better, a million tons of rain
Came swirling thro' the section by dug-out sap and drain.
Headquarters, store and cook-house, bomb-shelter, splinter-
    proof,
Were all filled up with water, and in fell every roof.
Scummy and dark and icy, the torrent at a touch
Sucked in the greasy trench-walls that mocked the drowning
    clutch.
And now the land was covered, and now with choking breath
The wretched victims unawares stepped into hideous death.
Behind the up-flung parados—half buried in the slime,
Their fingers numb and useless—their rifles choked with grime,
Thro' thirty hours of darkness and twenty hours of day,
Foodless and drinkless (save the mark), a frozen handful lay.
My friends at home—at breakfast you saw a casual hint
Of half a quarter of the truth in seven lines of print.
But somewhere in the sullen sky that seemed to mock our woes
God saw my soldiers freeze and drown. It is enough. He knows.

                                    Frederic W. D. Bendall

A Night March

The sun has set and the wild dogs wake;
   Far in the hills the sheep bells sound;
     Klisali's seven lights are lit.
Frogs, brass-tongued, where the misty lake
   Merges slowly in marshy ground
     Jeer and cackle with vacant wit.
We from our scarce-pitched bivouac
   Take the road, as of old in France
     Alert we took it; mosquitoes dance
And shrill with delight up the vagabond track
   In the swirling dust; and the pipers play
     As our kilted company marches away.

Hard on our flank the Ilanli height
   Looks on the plain, and hems our view
     Of burning stars in a Balkan sky.
Low by the lake, thro' the odorous night,
   On a track that Persian and Roman knew,
     Strong-limbed, the Scottish Brigade streams by.
And to those that follow the pipes, what fate
   In the hidden days of the year shall come?
     Some shall see wounds and Scotland, some
By the Struma waters shall lie in state,
   Stricken of fever or foe; for them
     The cannon shall thunder a requiem.

                  John Macleod

Two Mornings

In Flanders where the soldiers lie,
   The mist-hung world is cheerless grey,
And willows watch with leaden eye
   Penurious dawn greet haggard Day.

Here on a sudden Night grows old,
   And in the gap between the hills,
Green, orange, amethyst, and gold
   The careless hand of morning spills.

                  Stuart Bellhouse

111

To Wingles Tower

I sit and gaze at Wingles
As the fading sunlight mingles
With the smoke that hangs o'er Hersin and Béthune.
For a moment Loos reposes
As another long day closes
And awaits the rising of another moon.

In the background Fosse's towers
Through the long and weary hours
Like a sentinel on guard above the mine,
And surveys the field of battle
Silent now save for the rattle
Of the wheels of transport going up the line.

On the right the long white trenches,
Waterlogged and full of stenches
Crawl like snakes across the Lens-La Bassée road,
Where the trees all bent and battered,
Seared with scars where shrapnel spattered,
Bow like aged men beneath a heavy load.

Silver clouds hang soft and dreamy
O'er the distant ridge of Vimy
Where the ruined hamlets snuggle down to rest.
Through the golden autumn glimmer
In the trees there steals the shimmer
Of the sun that sinks in flame into the west.
I have gazed on Wingles Tower
Hour after weary hour,
Till my heavy eyes ceased watching for a while,
And sometimes I fell to wondering
If I'd not been sorely blundering
When I thought I knew the meaning of your smile.

Vivian T. Pemberton

At a British Cemetery in Flanders

Here lie no mercenaries who for gold
   Bartered their strength and skill and their life's blood;
These men led homely lives, and looked to grow old
   In peace earning a quiet livelihood.
Yet when the drums made summons near and far
   They sprang to arms, pitifully unprepared
For the great agony of modern war;
   And here in Flanders with their comrades shared
Honour and pain, and here in Flanders died
   Unflinching . . . Weep a little and be content,
Strong in your faith and in your measureless pride.
   Their trial was great and their death excellent.

Digby B. Haseler

No Man's Land

Nine-thirty o'clock? Then over the top,
And mind to keep down when you see the flare
Of Very pistol searching the air.
Now, over you get; look out for the wire
In the borrow pit, and the empty tins,
They are meant for the Hun to bark his shins.
So keep well down and reserve your fire—
All over? Right: there's a gap just here
In the corkscrew wire, so just follow me;
If you keep well down there's nothing to fear.

. . . .

Then out we creep thro' the gathering gloom
Of NO MAN'S LAND, while the big guns boom
Right over our heads, and the rapid crack
Of the Lewis guns is answered back
By the German barking in the same refrain
Of crack, crack, crack, all over again.

To the wistful eye from the parapet,
In the smiling sun of a summer's day,

'Twere a sin to believe that a bloody death
In those waving grasses lurking lay.
But now, 'neath the Very's fitful flares
"Keep still, my lads, and freeze like hares;—
All right, carry on, for we're out to enquire
If our friend the Hun's got a gap in his wire;
So lift up your feet and follow me."

. . . .

Then, silent, we press with a noiseless tread
Thro' no man's land, but the sightless dead;
Aye, muffle your footsteps, well ye may,
For the mouldering corpses here decay
Whom no man owns but the King abhorred,
Grim Pluto, Stygia's over-lord.
Oh breathe a prayer for the sightless Dead
Who have bitten the dust 'neath the biting lead
Of the pitiless hail of the Maxim's fire,
'Neath the wash of shell in the well trod mire.
For we've come to the wire of our friend, the Hun.
"Now keep well down, lads; can you see any gap?

. . . .

Not much, well the reference is wrong on the map."
So homeward we go thro' the friendly night.
That covers the NO MAN'S LAND from sight,
As muttering a noiseless prayer of praise,
We drop from the parapet into the bays.

Robert H. Beckh

Youth in Arms

(I)

Happy boy, happy boy,
David the immortal willed,
Youth a thousand, thousand times

114

Slain, but not once killed,
Swaggering again today
In the old contemptuous way;
Leaning backwards from your thigh
Up against the tinselled bar—
Dust and ashes! Is it you?
Laughing, boasting, there you are!
In your modern avatar.

Soldier, rifle, brown khaki—
Is your blood as happy so?
Where's your sling or painted shield,
Helmet, pike, or bow?
Well, you're going to the wars—
That is all you need to know.
Greybeards plotted. They were sad.
Death was in their wrinkled eyes.
At their tables, with their maps,
Plans and calculations, wise
They all seemed; for well they knew
How ungrudgingly Youth dies.

At their green official baize
They debated all the night
Plans for your adventurous days
Which you followed with delight,
Youth in all your wanderings,
David of a thousand slings.

(IV)

Carrion

It is plain now what you are. Your head has dropped
Into a furrow. And the lovely curve
Of your strong leg has wasted and is propped
Against a ridge of the ploughed land's watery swerve.

You are swayed on waves of the silent ground;
You clutch and claim with passionate grasp of your fingers
The dip of earth in which your body lingers;
If you are not found,

115

In a little while your limbs will fall apart;
The birds will take some, but the earth will take most of
  your heart.

You are fuel for a coming spring if they leave you here;
The crop that will rise from your bones is healthy bread.
You died—we know you—without a word of fear,
And as they loved you living I love you dead.

No girl would kiss you. But then
No girls would ever kiss the earth
In the manner they hug the lips of men:
You are not known to them in this, your second birth.

No coffin-cover now will cram
Your body in a shell of lead;
Earth will not fall on you from the spade with a slam,
But will fold and enclose you slowly, you living dead.

Hush, I hear the guns. Are you still asleep?
Surely I saw you a little heave to reply.
I can hardly think you will not turn over and creep
Along the furrows trenchward as if to die.

Harold Monro

Trenches: St. Eloi

Over the flat slope of St. Eloi
A wide wall of sandbags.
Night.
In the silence desultory men
Pottering over small fires, cleaning their mess-tins:
To and fro, from the lines,
Men walk as on Piccadilly,
Making paths in the dark,
Through scattered dead horses,
Over a dead Belgian's belly.
The Germans have rockets. The English have no rockets.
Behind the line, cannon, hidden, lying back miles.
Before the line chaos:

My mind is a corridor. The minds about me are corridors.
Nothing suggests itself. There is nothing to do but keep on.

T. E. Hulme

Ghost of the Somme

A khaki phantom passed along the trench—
No one touched it, no one heard its step,
And yet it reeled along a duckboard track
Filled with widening eyes!
Was it a fiend from Hell
Come to join the Hell already there?
That Hell already there,
That Hell where trenches run like trains
Under a hail of red-hot steel
While crowded figures crouch
Waiting for steel to smash
The warrens of their watch!

At midnight in Loony Bin Lane
The line is lousy with loose steel
From bumping trench mortars!
Sandbags quake, men cower, and from world's other end
Stumbles this figure, eyeless for ever!
The sulphur stink, the black fumes, the blotted stars
And a handful of shrapnel have left it unseeing!

Helmet-less, the phantom holds its face
In two blind hands;
More terrible than the howling of multitudes
Is its strange blind silence!
From phantom fingers pressed against spectral face
Blood seems pouring down wrists,
Down dripping tunic, boots, puttees,
Yet no one hears its steps!

Reeling against the clay, it falls to earth
Still dabbling at the bloody mask,
The ghostly face!
Stretched on the long duckboards,

It seems to groan its last,
Fingers clenching and unclenching
Like a pleased cat!

We move to help it,
But we find nothing there,
No dying flesh, no drying blood, no carcass and no trace,
No evidence of what we've seen,
No witness of its death!
Not only soul but flesh and bones have fled
In agony to face
The blandishments of Hell!

Albert E. Tomlinson

Manslaughter Morning

On Manslaughter Morning in Massacre Wood
I see a sentry shoot his best friend's face away,
Cleaning his rifle at dawn stand-down.

They take him away with a sort of kind contempt,
A death among deathless deaths, a name among
    nameless names,
Duly reported to the ginger-haired captain.

In the Battle of the Somme
I see thirty khaki citizens
Carrying sandbags full of hand-bombs
Slung over khaki shoulders.
Resting on a green bank,
One citizen drops his bag carelessly
To rest on foreign clay.
The explosion blows his back out,
The small of his back out,
The small of his back and webbing and khaki!
I see his inside
Like an operating table model,
For he is dead but not quite dead,
And his limbs ache with war!

At midnight in murder time
Along Loony Bin Lane,
The Line is lousy with loose metal!
Sandbags quake, men cower and from world's outer end
Stumbles a figure, eyeless for ever!

Helmet-less, he tries to hold his face shreds
With both blind hands!
More terrible than multitudes howling
Is his last blind silence!
From fingers pressed against blood,
Blood comes pouring down his wrist,
Drenching boots, puttees, tunic;
Still dabbling at the petalled mask,
Once a man's face,
And stretched on the long duckboards,
He groans his last,
Fingers clenching and unclenching
Like a pleased cat!

Albert E. Tomlinson

The Death-Bed

He drowsed and was aware of silence heaped
Round him, unshaken as the steadfast walls;
Aqueous like floating rays of amber light,
Soaring and quivering in the wings of sleep.
Silence and safety; and his mortal shore
Lipped by the inward, moonless waves of death.

Someone was holding water to his mouth.
He swallowed, unresisting; moaned and dropped
Through crimson gloom to darkness; and forgot
The opiate throb and ache that was his wound.
    Water—calm, sliding green above the weir.
    Water—a sky-lit alley for his boat;
    Bird-voiced, and bordered with reflected flowers
    And shaken hues of summer; drifting down,
    He dipped contented oars, and sighed, and slept.

Night, with a gust of wind, was in the ward,
Blowing the curtain to a glimmering curve.
Night. He was blind; he could not see the stars
Glinting among the wraiths of wandering cloud;
Queer blots of colour, purple, scarlet, green,
Flickered and faded in his drowning eyes.

Rain—he could hear it rustling through the dark;
Fragrance and passionless music woven as one;
Warm rain on drooping roses; pattering showers
That soak the woods; not the harsh rain that sweeps
Behind the thunder, but a trickling peace,
Gently and slowly washing life away.

He stirred, shifting his body; then the pain
Leapt like a prowling beast, and gripped and tore
His groping dreams with grinding claws and fangs.
    But someone was beside him; soon he lay
    Shuddering because that evil thing had passed.
    And death, who'd stepped toward him, paused and stared.

Light many lamps and gather round his bed.
Lend him your eyes, warm blood, and will to live.
Speak to him, rouse him; you may save him yet.
He's young; he hated War; how should he die
When cruel old campaigners win safe through?

But death replied: 'I choose him.' So he went,
And there was silence in the summer night;
Silence and safety; and the veils of sleep.
Then far away, the thudding of the guns.

Siegfried Sassoon

Foot Inspection

The twilight barn was chinked with gleams; I saw
Soldiers with naked feet stretched on the straw,
Stiff-limbed from the long muddy march we'd done,
And ruddy-faced with April wind and sun.
With pity and stabbing tenderness I see

Those stupid, trustful eyes stare up at me.
Yet, while I stoop to Morgan's blistered toes
And ask about his boots, he never knows
How glad I'd be to die, if dying could set him free
From battles. Shyly grinning at my joke,
He pulls his grimy socks on; lights a smoke,
And thinks, 'Our officer's a decent bloke'.

Siegfried Sassoon

Prelude: The Troops

Dim, gradual thinning of the shapeless gloom
Shudders to drizzling daybreak that reveals
Disconsolate men who stamp their sodden boots
And turn dulled, sunken faces to the sky
Haggard and hopeless. They, who have beaten down
The stale despair of night, must now renew
Their desolation in the truth of dawn,
Murdering hours that grope for peace.

Yet these who cling to life with stubborn hands,
Can grin through storm of death and find a gap
In the clawed, cruel tangles of his defence.
They march from safety, and the bird-sung joy
Of grass-green thickets, to the land where all
Is ruin, and nothing blossoms but the sky
That hastens over them where they endure
Sad, smoking, flat horizons, reeking woods,
And foundered trench-lines volleying doom for doom.

O my brave brown companions, when your souls
Flock silently away, and the eyeless dead
Shame the wild beast of battle on the ridge,
Death will stand grieving in that field of war
Since your unvanquished hardihood is spent.
And through some mooned Valhalla there will pass
Battalions and Battalions, scarred from hell;
The unreturning army that was youth;
The legions who have suffered and are dust.

Siegfried Sassoon

How to Die

Dark clouds are smouldering into red
    While down the crater morning burns.
The dying soldier lifts his head
    To watch the glory that returns:
He lifts his fingers towards the skies
    Where holy brightness breaks in flames;
Radiance reflected in his eyes,
    And on his lips a whispered name.

You'd think, to hear some people talk,
    That lads go West with sobs and curses,
And sullen faces white as chalk,
    Hankering for wreaths and tombs and hearses.
But they've been taught the way to do it
    Like Christian soldiers; not without haste
And shuddering groans; but passing through it
    With due regard for decent taste.

                                Siegfried Sassoon

The Dug-Out

Why do you lie with your legs ungainly huddled,
And one arm bent across your sullen, cold
Exhausted face? It hurts my heart to watch you,
Deep-shadow'd from the candle's guttering gold;
And you wonder why I shake you by the shoulder;
Drowsy, you mumble and sigh and turn your head . . .
You are too young to fall asleep for ever;
And when you sleep you remind me of the dead.

                                Siegfried Sassoon

Counter-Attack

We'd gained our first objective hours before
While dawn broke like a face with blinking eyes,
Pallid, unshaven and thirsty, blind with smoke.
Things seemed all right at first. We held their line,
With bombers posted, Lewis guns well placed,
And clink of shovels deepening the shallow trench.
   The place was rotten with dead; green clumsy legs
   High-booted, sprawled and grovelled among the saps
   And trunks, face downwards, in the sucking mud,
   Wallowed like trodden sand-bags loosely filled,
   And naked sodden buttocks, mats of hair,
   Bulged, clotted heads slept in the plastering slime.
   And then the rain began,—the jolly old rain!

A yawning soldier knelt against the bank,
Staring across the morning blear with fog;
He wondered when the Allemands would get busy;
And then of course, they started with five-nines
Traversing, sure as fate, and never a dud.
Mute in the clamour of shells he watched them burst
Spouting dark earth and wire with gusts from hell,
While posturing giants dissolved in drifts of smoke.
He crouched and flinched, dizzy with galloping fear,
Sick for escape,—loathing the strangled horror
And butchered, frantic gestures of the dead.

An officer came blundering down the trench:
"Stand-to and man the fire-step!" On he went . . .
Gasping and bawling, "Fire-step . . . counter-attack!"
Then the haze lifted. Bombing on the right
Down the old sap: machine-guns on the left;
And stumbling figures looming out in front.
"O Christ, they're coming at us!" Bullets spat,
And he remembered his rifle . . . rapid fire . . .
And started blazing wildly . . . then a bang
Crumpled and spun him sideways, knocked him out
To grunt and wriggle: none heeded him; he choked
And fought the flapping veils of smothering gloom,
Lost in a blurred confusion of yells and groans . . .
Down, and down, and down, he sank and drowned,
Bleeding to death. The counter-attack had failed.

                                        Siegfried Sassoon

The Enemy

To Germany

You are blind like us. Your hurt no man designed,
And no man claimed the conquest of your land.
But gropers both through fields of thought confined
We stumble and we do not understand.
You only saw your future bigly planned,
And we, the tapering paths of our own mind,
And in each other's dearest ways we stand,
And hiss and hate. And the blind fight the blind.

When it is peace, then we may view again
With new-won eyes each other's truer form
And wonder. Grown more loving-kind and warm
We'll grasp firm hands and laugh at the old pain,
When it is peace. But until peace, the storm
The darkness and the thunder and the rain.

Charles H. Sorley

1914

He went without fears, went gaily, since go he must,
And drilled and sweated and sang, and rode in the heat and the
  dust
Of the summer; his fellows were round him, as eager as he.
While over the world the gloomy days of war dragged heavily.

He fell without a murmur in the noise of battle; found rest
'Midst the roar of hooves on the grass, a bullet struck through
  his breast.
Perhaps he drowsily lay; for him alone it was still,
And the blood ran out of his body, it had taken so little to kill.

So many thousand lay round him, it would need a poet, maybe,
Or a woman, or one of his kindred, to remember that none were
  as he;

127

It would need the mother he followed, or the girl he went beside
When he walked the paths of summer in the flush of his
   gladness and pride,

To know that he was not a unit, a pawn whose place can be
   filled;
Not blood, but the beautiful years of his coming life have been
   spilled,
The days that should have followed, a house and a home, maybe,
For a thousand may love and marry and nest, but so shall not
   he.

When the fires are alight in the meadow, the stars in the sky,
And the young moon drives its cattle, the clods graze silently,
When the cowherds answer each other and their horns sound
   loud and clear,
A thousand will hear them, but, he, who alone understood, will
   not hear.

His pale poor body is weak, his heart is still, and a dream
His longing, his hope, his sadness. He dies, his full years seem
Drooping palely around, they pass with his breath
Softly, as dreams have an end—it is not a violent death.

My days and the world's pass dully, our times are ill;
For men with labour are born, and men, without wishing it, kill.
Shadow and sunshine, twist a crown of thorns for my head!
Mourn, O my sisters! singly, for a hundred thousand dead.

Ferenc Békássy

Last Nocturne

   The search-light swords
Stab the sky
Miles back,
Light taut cords
Of gold, high
Against the black.

   A star-flare
Of showering red

Surprises the night,
And hangs in the air,
Painting the dead
With ruddy light.

    The pale wax
Of their faces
Turns to blood
By dim tracks
In dark places
Of the wood

    Where I go
Hurrying on.
Suddenly
I stumble low
On some one.
God on high!

    His face was very cold,
And very white;
There was no blood.
I grew old
That night
In the wood.

    He was young,
My enemy—
But lips the same
As lips have sung
Often with me.
I whispered the name

    Of the friend whose face
Was so like his;
But never a sound
In the dim place
Under the trees
Closing around.

    Then I cursed
My Nocturnes—
I hated night;

Hated it worst
When the moon turns
Her tired light

On horrible things
Man has done
With life and love.
Only a fool sings
When night's begun
And the moon's above.

I cursed each song
I made for men
Full of moonlight
Lasting night-long;
For I knew then
How evil is night.

I cursed each tune
Of night-dim wood
And Naiad's stream,
By that mad moon
A search for blood
And the waxen gleam

Of dead faces
Under the trees
In the trampled grass,
Till the bloody traces
Of the agonies
Of night-time pass.

Henry L. Simpson

The German Dug-Out

Forty feet down
A room dug out of the clay,
Roofed and strutted and tiled complete;
The floor still bears the mark of feet
(Feet that never will march again!),

The door-post's edge is rubbed and black
(Shoulders that never will lift a pack
Stooping through the wind and rain!),
Forty feet down from the light of day,
Forty feet down.

Ago
Sixteen men lived there,
Lived, and drank, and slept, and swore,
Smoked, and shivered, and cursed the war,
Wrote to the people at home maybe,
While the rafters shook to the thudding guns;
Husbands, fathers, and only sons,
Sixteen fellows like you and me
Lived in that cavern twelve feet square
A week ago.

Into the dark
Did a cry ring out on the air
Or died they stiffly and unafraid
In the crash and flame of the hand-grenade?
We took the trench and its mounded dead,
And the tale of their end is buried deep,
A secret which sixteen corpses keep
With the sixteen souls which gasped and fled
Up forty steps of battered stair,
Into the dark.

Forty feet down,
Veiled from the decent sky,
The clay of them turns to its native clay,
And the stench is a blot on the face of the day.
Men are a murderous breed, it seems,
And these, maybe, are quieter so;
Their spirits have gone where such things go;
Nor worms nor wars can trouble their dreams;
And their sixteen twisted bodies lie
Forty feet down.

John L. C. Brown

To German Soldiers

I
Overture

As we curse not the car for the smash-up, but the lout at the
  lever controls;
So khakimen curse only quitters, and field-grey bears not their
  grudge;
As funkermen snot you with untruths, one fighterman voice
  shall troll
A salt-fresh rune, like a headland to square-face the
  funkerman's sludge.

II
Field-Grey Fightermen

As the Dutchman is bold for his heart, as the Cossack and Kurd
  for rapine,
So the Grey glues its back to the block-house, though
  skewbanked and stalled,
Sharing the sport of the killermen, sharing the right of the line,
Swinging no lead nor miking when the roster of courage is
  called.

Electric beavers of boudoirs, and sumptous lovers of saps;
The sob of the soddish minny arrests not your sedulous spade;
For you, from your mouldy shoon to the crop in your red-ringed
  caps,
Are merlin-pioneers and moles of the sand-bag shades.

III
Fightermen: Wrightermen

Home-press, foe-press, they're pimps and they're ponces of
  gamboge lies;
Their insults are stink, and their praises prussic for you in your
  rage
Of war, you fightermen in the fight, for you that despise
These fly-blown critics and liars, and the printed manure of
  page.

For years you've free-traded fatality, and paid to the perishing
  guns,

132

That spray such juice on the sandbags, cracking your skulls like
    cane;
Four, and your masters still slash you, you myriad surplus sons,
Like gads on the steaming river, like locust pests on the plain.

Four summers, from Liège to Langemarck, the field-grey has
    thriven on lead—
Four springs has the grey goose flown from Stornaway, North to
    the floes—
If Verdun's the vale of Gehenna, the Somme has seen one or two
    dead,
Khaki and grey together, ripe carrion for killerman 'shows'.

As crump-hole differs from crump-hole, as mire may be softer
    than mire,
As the cut of their tunics won't help much when the men are
    maimed yet alive,
So killerman Grey and killerman Drab are oafs of one sire,
Settling problems of population with Mills, Number Five.

IV
Turning Worms

The bear that dreamed through the cyclone will waken to
    cyclone the pine:
So will you, though mute through War's mistral, blaspheme
    when they cry for calm;
Then the gun-trail shall turn in the trench, and the breech shall
    make mistrals to whine,
Lament for the masters who sounded the killermen's tattoo to
    arm.

They were flung like putrescence, or stalks, to the middened
    field.
Field-grey and field-khaki, field fellows, articled mates of the
    kill;
They shall turn that trade on their tyrants, and richmen shall
    richly yield
Offal and life for the killerman, craving their sustenant swill.

The curtain falls, but the killerman keeps to his chaos track;
Stampedes that land that bore him, tumults the towns of his
    birth;

133

Until ancestral dazzle-lace generals pay bloodily back
Youth to the young, love to the lovers, hope to the earth.

Albert E. Tomlinson
(Richmond, Spring 1918)

Homoeopathy

"A great outburst of popular indignation." —Press, Passim, after
the anti-German riots.

"Trouncing the Teuton." —*Evening News*, Headline.

"We are heartily glad that the Russians burned Memel, and we
hope that the Allies will burn a good many more German towns
before this war is over." —*Morning Post*, Leading Article.

We was in the 'Blue Dragon', Sid 'Awkins and me,
When all of a sudden, "Here, Ernie," says he,
"There are limits to what flesh and blood can endure;
We must really protest against Prussian Kultur.
There's an alien butcher down Wapping High Street,
The swine's gone and asked me to pay for my meat;
His father's a Frenchman, his mother's a Moor,
But he'd do with a lesson in Prussian Kultur."

So we off like a streak, and we pulled him from bed,
And tore off his nightshirt and pummelled his head,
And rolled him along in the mud to secure
He should quite grasp the meaning of Prussian Kultur.

O the way that we bashed 'im and hooted and hissed
Was a sight Lady Bathurst ought not to have missed;
For her organ *Die Post* gives a steady and sure
Support to the tenets of Prussian Kultur.

Then we emptied the shop in a white moral heat,
I got half a bullock, my wife some pigs' feet,
And some very nice tripe which she thought ought to cure
The Kaiser's devotion to Prussian Kultur.

Yes, even the coppers themselves took a part
With a cutlet apiece from Sid 'Awkins's cart,
As a positive proof that they shared in our feeling,
And did not confuse moral protest with stealing.

Reassured by these kindly, encouraging cops,
We protested at each of the neighbouring shops,
Till at last at the end of our punitive week
They took us, pro forma, in front of the beak.

But he only remarked that no civilised nation
Could hope to withstand such extreme provocation.
"You're discharged, for I know that your motives were pure—
You desired to protest against Prussian Kultur!"

Grand Chorus

So fill up the cup and fill up the can!
A tradesman's a Hun and a copper's a man;
But O that each restaurateur were a brewer,
For a healthy great thirst has our British Kultur.

J. C. Squire

Tom

Tom he lay in No Man's Land with a bloody broken thigh,
Tom lay out among the wire and stared up at the sky.
The sun beat down like fire of hell and the earth was brown
   and dry.

Tom shouted out for water while the earth called out for rain,
And six good men went out to try and bring him in again,
And six good men lie deaf and blind upon that bloody plain.

But the Boche they wouldn't shoot at Tom, they liked to see
   him lie
Calling "Christ!" with burning lips and staring at the sky.
So Tom he lay in No Man's Land until he had to die.

Digby B. Haseler

Enemies

He stood alone in some queer sunless place
Where Armageddon ends; perhaps he longed
For days he might have lived; but his young face
Gazed forth untroubled; and suddenly there thronged
Round him the hulking Germans that I shot
When for his death my brooding rage was hot.

He stared at them half-wondering; and then
They told him how I'd killed them for his sake, —
Those patient, stupid, sullen ghosts of men;
And still there seemed no answer he could make.
At last he turned and smiled, and all was well
Because his face could lead them out of hell.

Siegfried Sassoon

The Effect

The effect of our bombardment was terrific. One man told me he
had never seen so many dead before. —War Correspondent.

'He'd never seen so many dead before.'
They sprawled in yellow daylight while he swore
And gasped and lugged his everlasting load
Of bombs along what once had been a road.
'How peaceful are the dead.'
Who put that silly gag in someone's head?

'He'd never seen so many dead before.'
The lilting words danced up and down his brain,
While corpses jumped and capered in the rain.
No, no; he couldn't count them any more . . .
The dead have done with pain:
They've choked; they can't come back to life again.

When Dick was killed last week he looked like that,
Flapping along the fire-step like a fish,

136

After the blazing crump had knocked him flat . . .
'How many dead? As many as ever you wish.
Don't count 'em; they're too many.
Who'll buy my nice fresh corpses, two a penny?'

Siegfried Sassoon

Hope

Billets

Green fields that are scented and sweet,
God's sunshine, the air, and the trees;
Thy beauties we knew not before,
They were there, and who doubts them that sees?

But we, who bereft for a space
Of the joys that God meant us to share,
Have been living 'mid sandbags, and scorched
Without shade from the sun's ceaseless glare.

Great God! How to welcome the day
When the Trenches are left, and the trees
Promise hopes of a respite from heat,
And from breath-stifling odours release.

For how long? Just four days is the span:
And how fleeting yet heav'n born it seems—
Then again to the Trenches, our goal,
And to plan for the Peace of our dreams.

                              Robert H. Beckh

Battle Hymn

Lord God of battle and of pain,
Of triumph and defeat,
Our human pride, our strength's disdain
Judge from Thy mercy-seat;
Turn Thou our blows of bitter death
To Thine appointed end;
Open our eyes to see beneath
Each honest foe a friend.

141

Give us to fight with banners bright
And flaming swords of faith;
We pray Thee to maintain Thy right
In face of hell or death.

Smile thou upon our arms, and bless
Our colours in the field,
Add Thou, to righteous aims, success
With peace and mercy seal'd.
Father and Lord of friend and foe
All-seeing and all-wise,
Thy balm to dying hearts bestow,
Thy sight to sightless eyes;
To the dear dead give life, where pain
And death no more dismay,
Where, amid Love's long terrorless Reign,
All tears are wiped away.

Donald F. G. Johnson

Reims

Thy altars smoulder, yet if Europe's tears
Can stay the doom of malice, they are thine
To quench the fires that lick thy sacred shrine,
And scar the treasure of thy glorious years.
And nought can salve the heart's despairing fears
That knows its Head dishonour'd, while rapine
Thunders upon His citadel divine,
Till all its ancient splendour disappears.
But courage, tho' no hand can raise again
Thy perish'd glories, garlanded by Time,
The arm yet faileth not that ruleth all,
And God himself the guilty shall arraign,
Bidding them answer their inhuman crime
Before his everlasting doom shall fail.

Donald F. G. Johnson

Youth and War

Among the windy spaces
The star-buds grow to light;
With pale and weeping faces
The day-hours bow to night;
Where down the gusty valleys
A blast of thunder dies,
And in the forest alleys
A startled night-bird cries.

No pain but bitter pleasure
Surrounds my spirit here,
For life's supernal treasure
Is garlanded with fear;
Bright trees delight the garden
About my love's bright home
But all the flower-roots harden
Under the frost of doom.

Like the bright stars above me
My youthful hopes were set;
Yearning for lips that love me;
O how can I forget
The boyish dreams that brought me
To the high azure gate
Of heaven, where beauty sought me,
And love was satiate?

Now honour lets me dally
No longer with desire,
But goads me to the valley
Of death, and pain, and fire;
Not love but hate constraining
The soldier in the field,
Honour alone remaining
Of virtue for a shield.

Yet who dare doubt, resigning
The joys that mortals prize—
Beyond the heart's repining,
Behind the sightless eyes—
For all the tears and anguish,

143

The piteous dismay—
True love at length shall vanquish,
And crown the dawning day?

Donald F. G. Johnson

And if a Bullet

And if a bullet in the midst of strife
Should still the pulse of this unquiet life,
'Twere well: be death an everlasting rest,
I oft could yearn for it, by cares opprest;
And be't a night that brings another day,
I still could go rejoicing on my way,
Desiring in no phantom heav'n to dwell,
Nor scared with terror of any phantom hell,
But gazing now I find not death a curse
Better than life perchance, at least not worse;
Only the fierce and rending agony,
The torment of the flesh about to die,
Affrights my soul; but that shall pass anon,
And death's repose or strife be found, that's gone;
Only with that last earthly ill to cope
God grant me strength, and I go forth with hope.

Alec C. V. de Candole

Optimism

At last there'll dawn the last of the long year,
    Of the long year that seemed to dream no end;
Whose every dawn but turned the world more drear,
    And slew some hope, or led away some friend.
Or be you dark, or buffeting, or blind,
We care not, day, but leave not death behind.

The hours that feed on war go heavy-hearted:
    Death is no fare wherewith to make hearts fain;
Oh, we are sick to find that they who started
    With glamour in their eyes come not again.

O Day, be long and heavy if you will,
But on our hopes set not a bitter heel.

For tiny hopes, like tiny flowers of Spring,
   Will come, though death and ruin hold the land;
Though storms may roar they may not break the wing
   Of the earthed lark whose song is ever bland.
Fell year unpitiful, slow days of scorn,
Your kind shall die, and sweeter days be born.

Alfred V. Ratcliffe

From a Flemish Graveyard

A year hence may pass the grass that waves
O'er English men in Flemish graves,
Coating this clay with green of peace
And softness of a year's increase,
Be kind and lithe as English grass
To bend and nod as the winds pass;
It was for grass on English hills
These bore too soon the last of ills.

And may the wind be brisk and clean,
And singing cheerfully between
The bents a pleasant-burdened song
To cheer these English dead along;
For English songs and English winds
Are they that breed these English minds.

And may the circumstantial trees
Dip, for these dead ones in the breeze,
And make for them their silver play
Of spangled boughs each shiny day.
Thus may these look above, and see
And hear the wind in grass and tree,
And watch a lark in heaven stand,
And think themselves in their own land.

Iolo A. Williams

From a Full Heart

In days of peace my fellow-men
　　Rightly regarded me as more like
A Bishop than a Major-Gen.,
　　And nothing since has made me warlike;
But when this age-long struggle ends
　　And I have seen the Allies dish up
The goose of HINDENBURG—oh, friends!
　　I shall out-bish the mildest Bishop.

When the War is over and the KAISER'S out of print,
I'm going to buy some tortoises and watch the beggars sprint;
When the War is over and the sword at last we sheathe,
I'm going to keep a jelly-fish and listen to it breathe.

I never really longed for gore,
　　And any taste for red corpuscles
That lingered with me left before
　　The German troops had entered Brussels.
In early days the Colonel's 'Shun!'
　　Froze me; and, as the War grew older,
The noise of someone else's gun
　　Left me considerably colder.

When the War is over and the battle has been won,
I'm going to buy a barnacle and take it for a run;
When the War is over and the German fleet we sink,
I'm going to keep a silk-worm's egg and listen to it think.

The Captains and the Kings depart—
　　It may be so, but not lieutenants;
Dawn after weary dawn I start
　　The never-ending round of penance;
One rock amid the welter stands
　　On which my gaze is fixed intently—
An after life in quiet hands
　　Lived very lazily and gently.

When the War is over and we've done the Belgians proud,
I'm going to keep a chrysalis and read to it aloud;
When the War is over and we've finished up the show,
I'm going to plant a lemon pip and listen to it grow.

Oh, I'm tired of the noise and the turmoil of battle,
And I'm even upset by the lowing of cattle,
And the clang of the bluebells is death to my liver
And the roar of the dandelion gives me a shiver,
And a glacier, in movement, is much too exciting
And I'm nervous, when standing on one, of alighting—
Give me Peace; that is all, that is all that I seek . . .
   Say, starting on Saturday week.

A. A. Milne

Stray Leaves

As I tramped off to join the fight
   A blackbird nodded to me—so!
Said, 'Hope we'll see you back all right.
   Keep safe. Cheero!

We carried all before us in the attack,
Broke through their lines and captured all the town—
A splendid victory! But we buried Jack
At Dead Man's Corner when the sun went down.

For my first night in a strange bed
I toss and turn and restless lie,
While cruel dreams chase through my head
And hideous forms go laughing by.

Tell me, brothers, how shall I fare
When the good body strong and brave
Sleeps with Death, and cold and bare
I spend my first night in the grave?

If I must die write not, " 'Tis sweet
   To fall for England in the fray."

But write, "Non omnis periit.
　Sed miles sed pro patria."
And add this one short line that fits—
"Gentlemen, when the barrage lifts . . ."

For O, it must be hard to die
　And leave the best of life behind
To lie beneath an alien sky
　Unknown, untended, hard to find.
To leave earth's red and green and gold
And turn to a little bitter mould.

Digby B. Haseler

In Billets

1917

The morning air is fresh and cool
Beside the willow-shaded pool,
And I can dream the hours away
At least for this long summer day,
And in my day-dreams I can see
A happier summer that shall be
When the torn earth has found release
From torture 'neath the wings of Peace.
Oh—on that longed-for summer day
Will there be flowers in Bernafay?
And shall I find the uncrumpling fern
Along the banks at Hébuterne?
Will the June roses scent the air
In the lost garden-lands of Serre,
And primroses again make good
The tangled depths of Delville Wood?
Will wind-flowers hide the whitened bones
That made a charnel-house of Trônes,
And Ginchy—levelled to the earth—
Spring in white blossom to new birth?
Will the blood shed at La Bassée
Give colour to the budding may,
And silver lilies sweetly tell

Of stainless lives lost at Gavrelle?
Surely some deathless mignonette
Will come again at Courcelette,
And scarlet poppies flutter on
The wind-swept cornfields of Péronne,
White seas of cherry-blossom foam
About the orchards of Bapaume,
And clover once again make fair
The sunlit uplands of Santerre.
Oh yes. I see them in my dreams
By Somme's cool swallow-haunted streams.
And sure am I that without fail
Seed-time and harvest shall prevail
To twine green garlands that will wave
Over the bodies of the brave,
And make the golden wheat-ears dance
Above the battle-fields of France.

                              Frederic W.D. Bendall

Stretcher Case

(To Edward Marsh)

He woke; the clank and racket of the train
Kept time with angry throbbings in his brain.
Then for a while he lapsed and drowsed again.
At last he lifted his bewildered eyes
And blinked, and rolled them sidelong; hills and skies,
Heavily wooded, hot with August haze,
And, slipping backward, golden for his gaze,
Acres of harvest.

Feebly now he drags
Exhausted ego back from glooms and quags
And blasting tumult, terror, hurtling glare,
To calm and brightness, havens of sweet air.
He sighed, confused; then drew a cautious breath;
This level journeying was no ride through death.
'If I were dead', he mused, 'there'd be no thinking—
And hueless, shifting welter where I'd drown.'
Then he remembered that his name was Brown.

But was he back in Blighty? Slow he turned,
Till in his heart thanksgiving leapt and burned.
Then shone the blue serene, the prosperous land,
Trees, cows and hedges; skipping these, he scanned
Large, friendly names, that change not with the year,
Lung Tonic, Mustard, Liver Pills and Beer.

Siegfried Sassoon

Comradeship

Two Nights

The moon's rim
Was over the wood,
As I trod with him
The quiet road.

The trees by the pond
Were still as stone;
The trees beyond
Were all alone.

Darkness clung
On the whole place;
A gleam swung
On the water's face.

And we talked of things
Of the dead days—
Forgotten stings,
Forgotten praise—

Till the sundered threads
Were all bound,
And the old gods' heads
Were all crowned . . .

As a sudden star
Stabs the night,
There came afar
The burden light

Of some mean song—
Before I knew
I stood among
The men, with you.

The moon was high
Over us then;
Suddenly
One of the men

Started to sing
Low, very low,
That same thing
Had moved me so.

So for an hour
I stood at your side;
The moon was a still flower,
And the guns cried.

We did not speak much;
At the latter end
For a moment, the touch
Of a warm hand,

And the calm look
Of quiet eyes—
These things spoke . . .
(God! if he dies.)

I turned and said,
'We'd better go;
(God! if he's dead)
Time hurries so.'

Henry L. Simpson

Night at Gomonic

Great, dark hills to the Westward rise,
Where star-strewn Lake Langaza lies
Beneath the violet Balkan skies.

Somewhere beyond those hills is he
Who lived and laboured and laughed with me.

Look! many glimmering camp-fires fret
The dark hills. So in my mind are set
Gold-sparkling times since first we met—

That raft—that midnight patrol—that ride
Over the holly-green countryside—

Erquinghem—Proyart—Hooge—Marseilles—
Billets and trenches—and English mails—
The sea—Greek villages—and nightingales—

Fierce Macedonian blizzards—Spring
With beauty the gaunt hills carpeting—
The cattle bells, when sleep was near,
Heard in the warm dusk, low and clear,
By the meadowy banks of the Iridere—

Dawn—and the eagles' lordly flight—
And wild geese clamouring in the night—

In those days fury nor fear, let slip
Tho' it were by hell, the delight could strip
From youth's war-conquering comradeship.

John Macleod

Outposts

Sentry, sentry, what did you see
At gaze from your post beside Lone Tree?
A star-shell flared like a burning brand
But I saw no movement in No Man's Land.
Sentry, sentry, what did you hear
As the night-wind fluttered the grasses near?
I heard a rifle-shot on the flank,
And my mate slid down to the foot of the bank.

Sentry, sentry, what did you do?
And hadn't your mate a word for you?
I lifted his head and called his name.
His lips moved once, but no sound came.

Sentry, sentry, what did you say
As you watched alone till break of day?
I prayed the Lord that I'd fire straight
If I saw the man that killed my mate.

Frederic W. D. Bendall

The Triumph

When life was a cobweb of stars for Beauty who came
  In the whisper of leaves or a bird's lone cry in the glen,
On dawn-lit hills and horizons girdled with flame
  I sought for the triumph that troubles the faces of men.

With death in the terrible flickering gloom of the fight
  I was cruel, and fierce with despair; I was naked and bound;
I was stricken: and Beauty returned through the shambles of night;
  In the faces of men she returned; and their triumph I found.

Siegfried Sassoon

From an Untitled Poem

Light-lipped and singing press we hard
Over old earth which now is worn,
Triumphant, buffeted and scarred,
By billows howled at, tempest-torn,
Toward blue horizons far away
(Which do not give the rest we need,
But some long strife, more than this play,
Some task that will be stern indeed)—
We ever new, we ever young,
We happy creatures of a day!
What will the gods say, seeing us strung
As nobly and as taut as they?

Charles H. Sorley

156

Their Friendship Was Mine

Who shall I praise for the days of my warring?
Who shall I thank for the friends at my side?
For there may be a god or there may be an ending,
But these men were men who fought there and died.

Their's was the friendship of glorious laughter;
They laughed at their wounds with their dying breath,
The pomp of the world and its prizes they laughed at,
Laughing at life as they laughed at death.

Their's was the flame and their's was the heritage,
Their's was the excellent scourging of war;
The slain were their's and also the slaughter,
Honour them, then, for the burdens they bore.

Honour them not as ye honour those others,
The successes of peace, or the stalwarts of trade;
Generations of peace have to be paid for,
Their's was the generation that paid.

Not for a coin nor yet for possessions
Those fools kept their compact up there in the line;
Their own self-respect was the whole of their profit,
Their folly I shared and their friendship was mine.

What is there in life that makes it worth keeping?
Only the courage to lose it at call,
Only the thought that you gave without whining
The answer of men to the last call of all.

To them came the call of the world in its warring,
Workman and farmer, shopman and clerk,
Their friendship was mine as they marched with their answer
From life in its sweetness into the dark.

Albert E. Tomlinson

Men of the Line

Men of the line, their friendship is mine,
Friendship forced on rats in a trench,
The day has no night, night has no song
Save a handful of earth and a skinful of stench!

Men of the line whose friendship is mine,
The trench is our High Street, our town and our bed,
Through a persicope paradise staring at death.
Friendship is there though no word is said.

Our is the friendship of suffering and laughter,
Some laugh, some weep with vultured breath,
Unsellable souls that pass through the sales ring,
Sugar meat of battle in shops of death.

The clarion of cash is not one they answer,
For a franc per fool they hold on to the line,
These very civilian soldiers of quality—
Their ditch I share and their friendship is mine.
Their's is the hell and their's is the heritage,
These manhole midgets of modern war,
The slain are their's and also the slaughter,
Spare pity-dust then for the burden they bear.

Forget them not as forgotten these others,
The picked men of peace, the ditch-troops of trade,
Generations of peace have to be paid for,
This is one generation that paid!

What can life give to make it worth buying?
Only the courage to lose it at call—
Like dogs in a ditch they gave without whining
The answer of men to the last call of all.

Men of the line and the lean strength within them,
A pennorth of ploughman, a haporth of clerk,
Their friendship is mine, dear God, and the answer
That mouths without platforms give to the dark!

Albert E. Tomlinson

To a Fallen Comrade

You came to us fresh from school, bright-eyed,
　With clear young voice that brought new zest
To hearts grown sick with hope denied,
　To limbs that were worn and craved for rest.
The Vision Splendid beckoned you;
　Spring spurr'd your ready step; your breath
Quickened with eagerness to view
　Your life's fair highway, scorning death.

For many months with us you stayed,
　Fought with us, toiled with us, shared our food.
The Vision Splendid did not fade;
　Right still was might and God was good.
And when we laughed and spoke of Fate,
　(That fought against us), death and wounds,—
Doubt was for cowards! Death a gate
　That led to happier hunting grounds!

Ah well! You passed that gateway through!
　Passed in a shroud of smoke and flame. . . .
And all that we could find of you,—
　Of your white limbs, of your young frame,
We gathered up into a sack
　And bore to a quiet resting-place;
Then strove, as again we faced the track
　Of trenchboards, to forget your face.

Yet in the dusk I see your eyes,
　True still and tender; glorying
In Youth's gay quest,—or sacrifice
　With whate'er fate the day might bring.
Your life's fair highway, sunn'd by hope,
　Ends at a rough-hewn wooden cross!
In the eternal horoscope
　What is of gain? And what of loss?

Youth's pulsing blood 'twas yours to yield
　Even as you woke to find its power,
And laughter in the playing-field,
　Joy in the saddle,—all the dower
Of your young manhood! More than these,
　Your spirit's need of sense resigned;—

159

Moonlight that floods a world of trees,
  Melody vibrant on the wind!

The sweet elusive scent that slips
  From out a cloud of dusky hair,
The soft allure of laughing lips
  You never knew; nor felt the rare
Sweet flame of Passion make demands
  That broken be the bolts and bars;—
Till Love, with her curbing, pitying hands,
  Lifts the bruised spirit to the stars.

Somewhere still dwells your spirit's mate,
  Body for body, soul for soul!
Not yours to find her! God (or Fate,—
  I still must mock you) rent the scroll
Too soon and surely; and no view
  Of Immortality was shown
In infant lips to lisp for you,
  In little steps beside your own.

All these you lost; for recompense,
  The bonds of comradeship were yours,
The thrill of waiting for the tense,
  Clean joys of danger, and the hours,
Twice precious, when one rests again,
  Drawing new strength with every breath,—
And the blind worship of your men,
  Your dumb, proud followers to death.

'Tis better so! Before you lies
  No fetid life on office stool,
Compassed with trivial compromise
  To clog your spirit, ever full
Of joys forbidden, hope delayed,
  Love that grows grey and turns to lust,
Of buds that blossom but to fade
  And gods that crumble into dust.

These cannot reach you, but the path
  Of truth and honour, this you knew.
Living, you raised aloft your faith,
  Dying, you laughed to find it true.

160

Living, you clutched each sand of Time,
    Drank from the golden cup your fill.
Dying, you yielded in their prime
    Body and spirit, spotless still.

Gladly you heard the echoing horn
    Call to those happier hunting-grounds;
And kind hands led you to your bourne,
    Doffed your worn armour, cleansed your wounds.
We, whose blood ran with yours to swell
    The stain on Earth's great palimpsest,
Rise to salute you. Fare you well!
    Ours to remember, yours to rest.

                                    Geoffrey Fyson

No-Man's Land

After the long weeks, my son, we meet at last.
The times have gone above us both so fast—so fast
That but an eyelid's fall would seem to span
The years that changed you from a boy to man . . .
You with the blossom-face, and eyes of wonder,
Blue as the strange new skies you wandered under,
All was so fresh to you—the world a toy—
Vivid, bewildering, delightful boy . . .
You with new knowledge and the heart of youth
For ever seeking the eternal Truth . . .
Child—boy—man—all that my heart held dear—
All that was You—except the soul—lies here.

So strangely still! And I to see your face
Must creep in darkness to this fateful place,
The dreadful midst, where but to raise a head
Will add another to the unburied dead,
Where noiselessly a dozen yards away
Nerve-shattered men await the dawning day,
And search, with fingers twitching on their triggers,
For fancied forms and fear-created figures.

Ah, you are wise and quiet! Saner far
Than these poor shaken desperate creatures are,

161

Or I, who crouch beneath the scudding sky
Ready to kill, or, failing that, to die,
Flattening myself like any hunted hare
Beneath the moonlight and the star-shell's flare.
God! Has the world gone mad that men should creep
To slay an unknown brother in his sleep!
This silent congregation is more wise
Than all live things which crawl beneath the skies.

Gropingly in the dark my fingers trace
Each feature of the well-remembered face . . .
The firm young mouth, straight nose, and boyish brow,
The eyes whose wonderment is over now
(The night lies heavy on their dawning blue);
For the last time I run my fingers through
The fair young locks, sun-kissed and touched to gold . . .
For the last time my fingers find and hold
Those strong young fingers, now so cold—so cold!
A week, my son, I sought the place you fell;
Now I have found you. Greeting and farewell!

O God, whose Son was mangled on a tree,
By my poor mangled son I pray to Thee:
Let peace and pity ring this earth about,
Or send Thy thunderbolts and blot us out!

John L. C. Brown

Fragment: I strayed about the deck

I strayed about the deck, an hour, tonight
Under a cloudy moonless sky; and peeped
In at the window, watched my friends at table,
Or playing cards, or standing in the doorway,
Or coming out into the darkness. Still
No one could see me.

              I would have thought of them
—Heedless, within a week of battle—in pity,
Pride in their strength and in the weight and firmness
And link'd beauty of bodies, and pity that

162

This gay machine of splendour'ld soon be broken,
Thought little of, pashed, scattered. . . .

Only, always
I could see them—against the lamplight—pass
Like coloured shadows, thinner than filmy glass,
Slight bubbles, fainter than the wave's faint light,
That broke to phosphorus out in the night,
Perishing things and strange ghosts—soon to die
To other ghosts—this one, or that, or I.

Rupert Brooke
(April 1915)

Out of Battle

An Only Son's Dying Lament

I'm not a soldier born and bred,
I hate the sound of guns,
I joined because they told me
England needed all her sons.

I love old England's country scenes,
The old cliffs by the sea,
The peaceful, mist-clad Devon moors,
'Tis there that I would be.

I love the gentle English girls,
I love their graceful ways,
I love to watch the sheep dog's work,
And the lazy cattle graze.

They used to give me all I asked
In those dear old days of old,
They gave me wine, they gave me love,
And never asked for gold.

But now I do not ask for love,
For riches, wine, or song,
They tell me that I'll soon be well,
But I know they are wrong.

A stretcher-party brought me here,
My left leg hurts like sin,
They sent my pay-book and my gold
Back to my next of kin.

It is not much for which I ask,
I know my knell has rung,
But they will not give me anything
To cool my burning tongue.

Vivian T. Pemberton

Spreading Manure

There are forty steaming heaps in the one-tree field,
    Lying in four rows of ten,
They must be all spread out ere the earth will yield
    As it should (And it won't, even then).

Drive the great fork in, fling it out wide;
    Jerk it with a shoulder throw,
The stuff must lie even, two feet on each side.
    Not in patches, but level . . . so!

When the heap is thrown you must go all round
    And flatten it out with the spade,
It must lie quite close and trim till the ground
    Is like bread spread with marmalade.

The north-east wind stabs and cuts our breaths,
    The soaked clay numbs our feet,
We are palsied like people gripped by death
    In the beating of the frozen sleet.

I think no soldier is so cold as we,
    Sitting in the frozen mud.
I wish I was out there, for it might be
    A shell would burst to heat my blood.

I wish I was out there, for I should creep
    In my dug-out and hide my head,
I should feel no cold when they lay me deep
    To sleep in a six-foot bed.

I wish I was out there, and off the open land:
    A deep trench I could just endure.
But things being other, I needs must stand
    Frozen, and spread wet manure.

Rose Macaulay

Destroyers

On this primeval strip of western land,
With purple bays and tongues of shining sand,
Time, like an echoing tide,
Moves drowsily in idle ebb and flow;
The sunshine slumbers in the tangled grass
And homely folk with simple greeting pass
As to their worship or their work they go.
Man, earth and sea
Seem linked in elemental harmony
And my insurgent sorrow finds release
In dreams of peace.

But silent, grey,
Out of the curtained haze,
Across the bay
Two fierce destroyers glide with bows afoam
And predatory gaze,
Like cormorants that seek a submerged prey.
An angel of destruction guards the door
And keeps the peace of our ancestral home;
Freedom to dream, to work, and to adore,
These vagrant days, nights of untroubled breath,
Are bought with death.

Henry Head

Interval: Front Row Stalls

Over the footlights the ankles caper,
The grease paint glistens, the fringed eyes glance;
The last note shrills, and the curtain runs.

The man beside me opens a paper:
"Bitter weather—three mile advance—
Heavy losses—we take the guns."
And between my eyes and the crimson lights
Move the ranks of men who sat here o'nights,
And now lie heaped in the mud together,
Stiff and still in the bitter weather.

Kathleen Wallace

The Veteran

May, 1916

We came upon him sitting in the sun,
    Blinded by war, and left. And past the fence
There came young soldiers from the Hand and Flower,
    Asking advice of his experience.

And he said this and that, and told them tales,
    And all the nightmares of each empty head
Blew into the air; then hearing us beside,
    'Poor chaps, how'd they know what it's like', he said.

And we stood there, and watched him as he sat,
    Turning his sockets where they went away,
Until it came to one of us to ask
    'And you're—how old?'
    'Nineteen, the third of May.'

Margaret Postgate Cole

In Praise of Nurses

Are they not pure gold, our nurses?
(That's a crib from Browning, though!)
O for a Muse to write some verses
Worthy of them! Who would go

Troywards to lie at Helen's feet
When there's no maid so richly drest,
And there's no maid one half as sweet
As these with the Red Cross on their breast?

Maid of the reassuring glance
(The finest anodyne for pain)
How desolate a land were France
Without them kingdoms where you reign!

The kindly word the surgeons use
Shall not avail (at least not much)

While angels walk in nurses' shoes
And heaven greets us in their touch!

The hand that bears the nauseous drink
Hath fairer gifts than this in store,
That one should say, "I'm in the pink,
I don't think I'll need any more!"

Poor Helen was a frump to these,
And Cleopatra but a freak,
Let Tennyson say what he please
And Homer chaunt in ancient Greek!

But here's a query far above
All wisdom (save King Solomon's);
What shall I do now I'm in love
With twenty nurses all at once?

Digby B. Haseler

The Survivors

   We who came back,
Nerveless and maimed, from the wild sacrifice
Of the World's youth, stretch'd quivering on the rack
Of Nature pitiless to all its pain,
   Will never look again
With the old gay, uncomprehending eyes
Upon the former founts of our delight,
   Morning and eve and night,
Sunshine and shadow, melody, love, and mirth.
War tutored us too well. We know their worth,
   We who came back!

   These will recall
Our martyred innocence, the indelible stain
Of blood on our hands. Though leaves of coronal
Be heap'd upon our brows, 'twill not redress
   The eternal bitterness
That surges with the memory of our slain,
Our brothers by the bond of suffering.

And though the Spring
Lights with new loves the eyes that once were wet
For loss of them, WE never shall forget,
    We who came back!

Geoffrey Fyson

To a Pacifist

Do you fail, even now, to realize
That not for this, our land we hold most dear
Alone, nor for the freedom that we prize;
Not for the love that wells in loyal eyes
To nerve our spirits;—not alone, you hear.
For these;—but for yourself and for your breed,—
You, with your turgid soul and venomous tongue,
    You who have ever flung
    Gibes at our sacrifice,—
For you, too, must we suffer, must we bleed?

This thing is plain, altho' your lips deny;
When Honour calls,—for you we answer her;
When Death claims dues,—for you we go to die;
You thrive by virtue of our agony.
A saprophyte upon the sepulchre,
Lapping the spilt blood of the crucified,
This is your meed of thanks and recompense;—
    With pompous eloquence
    To prate interminably,
Sland'ring the sacred cause of those who died.

Geoffrey Fyson

The Army of the Dead

I dreamed that overhead
I saw in twilight grey
The Army of the Dead
Marching upon its way,
So still and passionless,

172

With faces so serene,
That scarcely could one guess
Such men in war had been.

No mark of hurt they bore,
Nor smoke, nor bloody stain,
Nor suffered any more
Famine, fatigue or pain;
Nor lust of any hate
Now lingered in their eyes—
Who have fulfilled their Fate
Have lost all enmities.

A new and greater pride
So quenched the pride of race
That foes marched side by side
Who once fought face to face.
That ghostly army's plan
Knows but one race, one rod—
All nations there are Men
And the one King is God.

No longer on their ears
The bugle's summons falls;
Beyond these tangled spheres
The Archangel's trumpet calls;
And by that trumpet led
Far up the exalted sky
The Army of the Dead
Goes by, and still goes by.

Look upward, standing mute;
  Salute!

Barry Pain

In Montauban

Quietly now, when the rush and roar of battle is over,
   In the wreck of the ruined shell-swept street he lies;
The pangs of death have left no mark but the jaw dropped open,
      And patient half-shut eyes.

Sixty winters have laid their joys and sorrows upon him,
   The hair is silvered which once was brown and thick,
And, near the hand which never shall grasp them living,
      Are placed a spade and pick.

Some old gardener, I fancy, who, back in his cottage in England,
   Read to his wife of a Sunday afternoon,
While the sun came through the blinds, and flowers were fragrant,
      And bees were loud in June.

Some old gardener, who, reading that hands were wanted,
   Strong and steady and cunning with pick and spade,
Dropped his paper, and went, his tools on his shoulder,
      Forth to follow his trade.

So for a time he laboured and hoed and mended,
   Stealing forth in the dusk when others sleep,
He and yeomen beside him, who work unknown, unnoticed,
      Making the trenches deep.

Then last night through the stars and silences, sudden
   A whistle and shattering crash like a thunder-roll,
And through the flying bricks, and the smoke, and the dust, uprising
      His startled kindly soul.

So, old friend, in the dawn you pass to a greater sunrise,
   Beyond the spite of men who mangle and slay;
And God, Who loves all gardeners, will greet you and bid you enter
      His sunnier ampler Day.

Widely and deep I dig, disposing the tools beside him,
   Crossing the toil-worn hands and propping the head,

And earth, whose fruits he honoured and worked for living,
    Rest on him lightly, dead.

                    John L. C. Brown

Bridging the Gulf; or, The Union of Classes

'On Wednesday a Bridge tournament was held at Sir ******'s
lovely house in Park Lane in aid of Lady *****'s fund for provid-
ing pure milk for the poor. The spacious rooms on the first floor
were filled with people.'—*The Observer*, 1915.

I

Sir Roger Trepan was a sensitive man, and very much moved by
the war.
It made him aware of a number of things he never had thought
of before.
He realized now he'd habitually left a rich man's obligations
neglected,
And he formed the conviction that this dereliction must
immediately be corrected.
"In my soul that was dead
  Comes a rushing of wind.
Peccavi!" he said,
  "I have sinned, I have sinned.
It's my duty", he said, "though these brigands
With their super-tax leave me half broke,
Now the country is slid, to brighten the squalid
Drab lives of less fortunate folk."

II

Sir Roger Trepan was a resolute man, the grass not under his
feet;
When he once had decided the course he must take he never
would own himself beat.
Aflame with his high patriotic resolve to show the morale of a
Bart.,
He embraced a career of deliberate devotion to England, and so
for a start
He ordered a lackey

To telephone through
To Jimmy and Jacky
  And Topsy van Boo
To request them to join him at dinner
And then come and watch Tree from a box,
That the Leeds unemployed might no more be annoyed
By the heart-rending shortage of socks.

III

Thenceforth—O the change, the miraculous change, from the
    thoughtless Sir Roger of old!—
With the strength of a saint and a statesman he ordered his
    most minute outlay of gold.
He could not be persuaded to buy a fur-coat, he would scarcely
    take tea with his aunt,
Without full satisfaction that each such transaction would
    benefit some one in want.
That His Majesty's lieges
  Should have a straight lead,
He ran a few gee-gees
  To keep up the breed,
And shot grouse for our poor wounded heroes
And danced for the Belgian Red Cross,
And took personal pains that our French friends' champagnes
Should not be produced at a loss.

IV

All hail to the war for the blessings it brings! And how could one
    estimate which
Are the greater, the gains that accrue to the poor or the benefits
    reaped by the rich?
For the poor now perceive that the rich, whom of old they
    regarded with baseless dislike,
Though they *seem* to be merely amusing themselves may be
    helping all classes alike.
If they act as trustees
  For the money they spend
The tangoest teas
  May bring fruit in the end,
And game-preserves, cars, and casinos, rightly handled, are
    sound as a bell,

And polo at Ranelagh may be not merely manly but socially
  useful as well.

V

And the rich. . . . Oh what prospects of service! What vistas of
  generous deeds!
They will never neglect, now they've found out a way, their poor
  fellow-citizens' needs.
They'll rejoice now they feel that they need never more of the
  ancient class-feeling be frightened,
That they've learnt during war to distinguish 'twixt pleasures
  which are, and which are not, enlightened.
They have opened their eyes,
  Though at very long last,
To their blind and unwise
  Lack of heart in the past,
And at last seen the sense of the Gospel
That they should not be selfish, like hogs,
That the Children may eat till they're round and replete,
But they *must* leave some crumbs for the dogs.

                        J. C. Squire

The Soul of a Nation

The little things of which we lately chattered—
  The dearth of taxis or the dawn of spring;
Themes we discussed as though they really mattered,
  Like rationed meat or raiders on the wing;—

How thin it seems to-day, this vacant prattle,
  Drowned by the thunder rolling in the West,
Voice of the great arbitrament of battle
  That puts our temper to the final test.

Thither our eyes are turned, our hearts are straining,
  Where those we love, whose courage laughs at fear,
Amid the storm of steel around them raining,
  Go to their death for all we hold most dear.

New-born of this supremest hour of trial,
  In quiet confidence shall be our strength,
Fixed on a faith that will not take denial
  Nor doubt that we have found our soul at length.

O England, staunch of nerve and strong of sinew,
  Best when you face the odds and stand at bay,
Now show a watching world what stuff is in you!
  Now make your soldiers proud of you to-day!

                                    28 March 1918

                                    Owen Seaman

War

1. Blood-Clap

Improvident man had farrowed and arrantly brought forth seed,
Sardined and machined and thick as flies on a sitfast sore,
Till the atrabilious earth grew clogged with her nasty breed,
And her engorged vessels broke in the sane blood-fury of War.

In cities, with fuss, had the Man-Ape forgotten his ancient Fear;
He was sure of the sun and childbirth, of bricks, and breeches
    and coal,
Of the snob-line barriers fixed 'twixt middleman, poor, and
    peer—
Then from the wilds of the gods and gorillas, War for his soul!—

Then from ado and declaiming, from clocks to the elbowed desk,
He 'listed along with Adventure, and frozenly slogged up the
    Line,
Where he proved that the panics of War are no more than a fool's
    burlesque;
Where his cheek robbed the brown from his butt, and its sights
    gave their glitter to his eyne.

2. Debility

As tape-worms nuzzle and fret and festoon in the slimes of our
    bile;

178

And as lice may bite or may suck, but the true louse invariably
   sucks,
As pollution will breed out pollution, and vileness manure but
   the vile,
So the squirms of Unfit in our midst were spawning the more for
   our mucks.

For babes that are born to Rolls-Royces will grow bellyslackly to
   hogs,
And wax on éclairs and harlots to the crispness and candour of
   dough,
So man to the gods seemed flabby and skint as an old aunt's
   dogs,
In the stews of Peace, and as straight as a stoat, and as clean as
   a crow.

As galvanic and wholesome he seemed as spittoons, and his
   whole life a clart,
With his rump jellybagged on a stool, his face a pudding-cloth
   souse,
With Stephen's and Stickfast for guts, and a district-season for
   heart,
And monotone, tinny typehammers his chords of Reveille and
   Rouse.

They fleshpotted him with puff-paste and music and marzipan,
And house-fugs and art and garlic, and salad-oil flabs in the
   neck;
On his kerbs the Daughters of Lot immemorially catered to
   Man,
And the squirms of a limpet race were sucking the races to
   wreck.

3. *Remedy*

So War from the Hammer-God North, came radio-active with
   shock,
And Man from Law of Barrage learned how piffling his law of
   Police,
From gambling of Guts how skemmily unclean his gambling of
   Stock,
And from stiff, green Dead in a dug-out the invertebrate slobber
   of Peace.

179

For War made zoomings and bombings, blew old things to Hell,
and scrapped
With a few drops of picric acid the antediluvian Past,
With the fading heats of first earth crackled the arrogance
wrapped
About Man, and breathed of the Utter Cold which will come at
the last.

Miasmas uncut of a thirty-foot sap breathed of troglodyte caves,
Fire-damps left by the guns breathed of dwellings on stilts in
lakes,
Death breathed its dews on bayonets, delirium breathed on the
Braves,
And some breathed their last on the mirror, for the health of
their honour's sake.

4. Upshot

Mothering is nails on the Cross, and Dying a fog, but War
Upheavals and makes amends; Life is a third-rate farce,
But War is as tame as a maelstrom, as mild as a tusking boar,
Its snarling of guns like the belling of wolves when the Winter's
sparse.

Nor is progress more than the muslin-wrap on the rawness of
meat!!—
Weeds of the culvert, claws of the Wild, and God's-image Man
Are the press at the Sixpenny-Gate, and the best bully gets the
seat,—
When birth has no achings, then War may cease from its arrière-
ban .

Albert E. Tomlinson

Banishment

I am banished from the patient men who fight.
They smote my heart to pity, built my pride.
Shoulder to aching shoulder, side by side,
They trudged away from life's broad wealds of light.
Their wrongs were mine; and ever in my sight

180

They went arrayed in honour. But they died,—
Not one by one: and mutinous I cried
To those who sent them out into the night.

The darkness tells how vainly I have striven
To free them from the pit where they must dwell
In outcast gloom convulsed and jagged and riven
By grappling guns. Love drove me to rebel.
Love drives me back to grope with them through hell;
And in their tortured eyes I stand forgiven.

Siegfried Sassoon

Sick Leave

When I'm asleep, dreaming and lulled and warm,—
They come, the homeless ones, the noiseless dead.
While the dim charging breakers of the storm
Bellow and drone and rumble overhead,
Out of the gloom they gather about my bed.
   They whisper to my heart; their thoughts are mine.
   'Why are you here with all your watches ended?
   From Ypres to Frise we sought you in the line.'
In bitter safety I awake, unfriended;
And while the dawn begins with slashing rain
I think of the Battalion in the mud.
'When are you going out to them again?
Are they not still your brothers through our blood?'

Siegfried Sassoon

Letter to Robert Graves

24 July 1918   American Red Cross Hospital, No. 22
                       98–99 Lancaster Gate, W.2

Dear Roberto,

I'd timed my death in action to the minute
(The *Nation* with my deathly verses in it).

The day told off—13—(the month July)—
The picture planned—O Threshold of the dark!
And then, the quivering songster failed to die
Because the bloody Bullet missed its mark.

Here I am; they *would* send me back—
Kind M.O. at Base; Sassoon's morale grown slack;
Swallowed all his proud high thoughts and acquiesced.
O Gate of Lancaster, O Blightyland the Blessed.

No visitors allowed
Since Friends arrived in crowd—
Jabber—Gesture—Jabber—Gesture—Nerves went phut and
failed
After the first afternoon when MarshMoonStreetMeiklejohn
    ArdoursandenduranSitwellitis prevailed,
Caused complications and set my brain a-hop;
Sleeplessexasperuicide, O Jesu make it stop!

But yesterday afternoon my reasoning Rivers ran solemnly in,
With peace in the pools of his spectacled eyes and a wisely
omnipotent grin;
And I fished in that steady grey stream and decided that I
After all am no longer the Worm that refuses to die.
But a gallant and glorious lyrical soldjer;
    Bolder and bolder; as he gets older;
    Shouting "Back to the Front
    For a scrimmaging Stunt."
    (I wish the weather wouldn't keep on getting colder.)

Yes, you can touch my Banker when you need him.
Why keep a Jewish friend unless you bleed him?

Oh yes, he's doing very well and sleeps from Two till Four.
And there was Jolly Otterleen a knocking at the door,
But Matron says she mustn't, not however loud she knocks
(Though she's bags of golden Daisies and some Raspberries in a
box),
Be admitted to the wonderful and wild and wobbly-witted
    sarcastic soldier-poet with a plaster on his crown,
Who pretends he doesn't know it (he's the Topic of the Town).

My God, my God, I'm so excited; I've just had a letter
From Stable who's commanding the Twenty-Fifth Battalion.

And my company, he tells me, doing better and better,
Pinched six Saxons after lunch,
And bagged machine-guns by the bunch.

But I—wasn't there—
O blast it isn't fair,
Because they'll all be wondering why
Dotty Captain wasn't standing by
When they came marching home.

But I don't care; I made them love me
Although they didn't want to do it, and I've sent them a glorious
Gramophone and God send you back to me
Over the green eviscerating sea—
And I'm ill and afraid to go back to them because those five-
nines are so damned awful.

When you think of them all bursting and you're lying on your
bed,
With the books you loved and longed for on the table; and your
head
All crammed with village verses about Daffodils and Geese—
. . . O Jesu make it cease. . . .

O Rivers please take me. And make me
Go back to the war till it break me.
Some day my brain will go BANG,
And they'll say what lovely faces were
The soldier-lads he sang

Does this break your heart? What do I care?

Sassons

Siegfried Sassoon

Loss and Remembrance

Cambridge in Wartime

Cambridge! Thou city of the hurrying feet,
  The nervous tread of palpitating youth,
Surging against thy walls in street and close,
  Eager in quest of pleasure, knowledge, truth;

Thou ancient cradle of a new-born age,
  Thy charm the mingling of the old and new,
The throbbing life amidst thy towers' decay,
  How changed, how sad, how pitiful to view,

Thine aspect now, beneath War's baneful spell!
  Thou art a mask, by wearer cast aside,—
A well gone dry,—a mother 'reft of child,
  Who mourning waits, with empty arms stretched wide.

No thronging youth in thy deserted courts,
  To wean us from the Past's far-reaching sway;
Back through the centuries our thoughts, Time's pawns,
  Unchallenged by the present, idly stray.

Our footsteps wander o'er forsaken lawns,
  Our lowered voices wake no answering tones,
With wisdom, truth and beauty in suspense,
  As if enchanted stand thy stately stones.

Cambridge! Thou art a city of the dead,
  The very reason of thy being fled.

Florence Edgar Hobson

Chestnut Sunday

From end to end of Cambridge town
The chestnut boughs move up and down,
And rain their petals on the grass
And on the busy folk who pass.

Their foaming sweetness drops in showers
Under a sky like gentian flowers;
White as a bride's is their array,
The chestnuts keeping holiday!

Oh, in your dreamless sleep, my dear,
I know, I know you see me here,
Between the voices and the sun,
And petals pattering, one by one.

I never feel you watch me weep,
Nor din of battle breaks your sleep,
But I am sure you woke this hour
To see your chestnut trees in flower!

                              Kathleen M. Wallace

Walnut-Tree Court

The court below drowns in an emerald deep
Of dusk, all murmurous
With things the river whispers in its sleep;
I, leaning outward thus
From this high window, over the silence, hear
Your voice, your laugh, and know
Down in the dusk, and infinitely near
You stand below. . . .

                              Kathleen M. Wallace

Yesterday

The winds are out tonight,
Strange winds, blown from a far-off troublous sea,
Rending the sky over the chimney pots,
Into a writhing web of jade and pearl—
And lashing my sedate black London trees
All into wonder and a breathless maze.

     I wonder if you hear?
From your still bed under Flanders soil,
I wonder if you know the winds are out?
For, if you do, I know across your sleep
There comes the dream that's tugging at my heart
Alone here with the lamplight and the fire,
And the day dying over London roofs:

     The thin white road
Leaping between the fenlands, where the sky
Swoops down to meet the fields, the flat brown fields,
With never a hill's curve, only poplar boughs
Like spires out of the mist at the day's edge.
And all the mad winds of the world full cry
Careering through the dusk into the town.

     And down the narrow streets,
Under the gray towers and serene gray walls,
Under the yellowing elms along the Backs,
The winds went rollicking and dancing still;
Swaying the chain of lights down King's Parade
And driving purple cloud-wrack down the sky
Running red flame behind the spires of King's.

     And so they came to us
Beating with wild wings in the court below,
Rocking the room, breaking the fire in gusts,
Filled with the spice of dead leaves and wet boughs,
Just as they come to me, alone, tonight.

. . . My dear, they say they will rebuild the world
Out of the soil where you and yours lie dead;
But not, I think, the free, the careless hours

That knew no shadow of purpose, but were glad,
When the glad winds raced under Cambridge walls.

Kathleen M.Wallace

Died of Wounds

Because you are dead, so many words they say,
If you could hear them, how they crowd, they crowd;
"Dying for England—but you must be proud"—
And "Greater love, honour, a debt to pay",
And "Cry, dear", someone says; and someone, "Pray!"
What do they mean, their words that throng so loud?

This, dearest; that for us there will not be
Laughter and joy of living dwindling cold,
Ashes of words that dropped in flame, first told;
Stale tenderness, made foolish suddenly.
This only, heart's desire, for you and me,
We who lived love, will not see love grow old.
We who had morning time and crest o' the wave
Will have no twilight chill after the gleam,
Nor any ebb-tide with a sluggish stream;
No, nor clutch wisdom as a thing to save.
We keep for ever (and yet they call me brave)
Untouched, unbroken, *unrebuilt*, our dream.

Kathleen M. Wallace

Unreturning

Under these walls and towers
   By these green water-ways,
Oh the good days were ours,
   The unforgotten days!

Too happy to be wise
   When the road used to run
Under such maddening skies

190

Headlong to Huntingdon.
Paths where the lilac spills
    Blossom too rich to bear;
Gold sheets of daffodils
    Lighting the Market Square;
    Shimmer of gliding prows
    Where the shade is cool,
Tea under orchard boughs,
    Smoke-rings by Byron's Pool.

Sunset at back of King's
    Behind the silver spire,
Talk of uncounted things
    Over a college fire—

Red leaves above your door,
    Gray walls and echoing street
Whose stones will never more
    Ring to your passing feet;

Strange! To think that Term is here,
    Life leads the same old dance,
While you lie dead, my dear,
    Somewhere in France. . . .

                    Kathleen M. Wallace

The Shadow

There was shadow on the moon: I saw it poise and tilt, and go
Its lonely way, and so I know that the blue velvet night will
    soon
Blaze loud and bright, as if the stars were crashing right into
    the town,
And tumbling streets and houses down, and smashing people
    like wine-jars. . . .

    Fear wakes:
    What then?
    Strayed shadow of the Fear that breaks
    The world's young men.

191

Bright fingers point all round the sky, they point and grope
  and cannot find.
(God's hand, you'd think, and he gone blind.) . . . The queer
  white faces twist and cry.
Last time they came they messed our square, and left it a hot
  rubbish-heap,
With people sunk in it so deep, you could not even hear them
  swear.

> *Fire blinds.*
> *What then?*
> *Pale shadow of the Pain that grinds*
> *The world's young men.*

The weak blood running down the street, oh, does it run like
  fire, like wine?
Are the spilt brains so keen, so fine, crushed limbs so swift,
  dead dreams so sweet?
There is a Plain where limbs and dreams and brains to set the
  world afire
Lie tossed in sodden heaps of mire. . . . Crash! Tonight's show
  begins, it seems.

> *Death . . . Well,*
> *What then?*
> *Rim of the shadow of the Hell*
> *Of the world's young men.*

Rose Macaulay

The Hero

"Jack fell as he'd have wished", the Mother said,
And folded up the letter that she'd read.
"The Colonel writes so nicely." Something broke
In the tired voice that quavered to a choke.
She half looked up. "We mothers are so proud
Of our dead soldiers." Then her face was bowed.

Quietly the Brother Officer went out.
He'd told the poor old dear some gallant lies

192

That she would nourish all her days, no doubt.
For while he coughed and mumbled, her weak eyes
Had shone with gentle triumph, brimmed with joy,
Because he'd been so brave, her glorious boy.
He thought how "Jack", cold-footed, useless swine,
Had panicked down the trench that night the mine
Went up at Wicked Corner; how he'd tried
To get sent home, and how, at last, he died,
Blown to small bits. And no one seemed to care
Except that lonely woman with white hair.

Siegfried Sassoon

Praematuri

When men are old and their friends die,
They are not so sad,
Because their love is running slow,
And cannot spring from the wound with so sharp a pain;
And they are happy with many memories,
And only a little while to be alone.

But we are young, and our friends are dead
Suddenly, and our quick love is torn in two;
So our memories are only hopes that came to nothing.
We are left alone like old men; we should be dead
—But there are years and years in which we shall still
   be young.

Margaret Postgate Cole

The Falling Leaves

November 1915

Today, as I rode by,
I saw the brown leaves dropping from their tree
In a still afternoon,
When no wind whirled them whistling to the sky,
But thickly, silently,

193

They fall, like snowflakes wiping out the noon;
And wandered slowly thence
For thinking of a gallant multitude
Which now all withering lay,
Slain by no wind of age or pestilence,
But in their beauty strewed
Like snowflakes falling on the Flemish clay.

Margaret Postgate Cole

Afterwards

Oh, my beloved, shall you and I
Ever be young again, be young again?
The people that were resigned said to me
—Peace will come and you will lie
Under the larches up in Sheer,
Sleeping
And eating strawberries and cream and cakes—
    O cakes, O cakes, O cakes, from Fuller's!
And quite forgetting there's a train to town,
Plotting in an afternoon the new curves for the world.

And peace came. And lying in Sheer
I look round at the corpses of the larches
Whom they slew to make pit-props
For mining the coal for the great armies.
And think, a pit-prop cannot move in the wind,
Nor have red manes hanging in spring from its branches,
And sap making the warm air sweet.
Though you planted it out on the hill again it would be dead.

And if these years have made you into a pit-prop,
To carry the twisting galleries of the world's reconstruction
(Where you may thank God, I suppose
That they set you the sole stay of a nasty corner)
What use is it to you? What use
To have your body lying here
In Sheer, underneath the larches?

Margaret Postgate Cole

New Year, 1916

Those that go down into silence. . . .

There is no silence in their going down,
  Although their grave-turf is not wet with tears,
Although Grief passes by them, and Renown
  Has garnered them no glory for the years.

The cloud of war moves on, and men forget
  That empires fall. We go our heedless ways
Unknowing still, uncaring still, and yet
  The very dust is clamorous with their praise.

                              Ada M. Harrison

The Poppies That Drop as I Watch

No charm nor loveliness nor joy is stable.
Glory unfolded for a world's delight
Fades like a lover's tale, a song, a fable
Blown over by the cruel breath of reason
And lost to sound and sight.
Beauty that burgeoned slowly through a season
Dies in a night.

For beauty dead we fill our hearts with weeping,
Yet never mark it pass beyond recall.
Shall only I, who once, like all men, sleeping
Felt not my gold transmute to baser metal,
With wakened eyes, see, bitterest of all,
Pale-hued and dark, petal by lovely petal
My silken poppies fall?

                              Ada M. Harrison

Missing: Unofficially Reported Killed

Was it noonday that you left us,
  When the ranks were wrapped in smoke?
Or did you pass unnoticed on the midnight,
  Ere the chillier morning broke?

Did the lust and heat of battle find you ready,
  Shoulders braced and heart aflame?
Or did death steal by and take you unexpected,
  When the final summons came?

Not amidst the companies and clamour
  Of this horror men call War,
Where man, the godlike, tramples down his fellows
  To the dust they were before;

But on some still November morning
  When the frost was in the air,
Noiselessly your strong soul took its passing,
  And I, your friend, not there—not there!
Silently the dead leaves swing and settle
  In their appointed place;
The season of the singing birds is over,
  The winter sets apace.

Somewhere in the ruin of the autumn,
  When the hosts of war are sped,
They will find you, 'midst the quiet wondering faces
  Of the unnumbered dead.

                              John L. C. Brown

The Dead Lover

Were you quick and active once—you that lie so still?
Did your brain run nimbly once, your lungs expand and fill?
Were problems worth the trying, was the living worth the dying?
Did the flying moment pay you for the labour up the hill?

Ah, you stay so silent now! You could tell me why
Woods are green in April now, and men are made to die.

Do you feel the spring, I wonder, through the turf you're sleeping
    under,
Though the thunder and the sunshine cannot reach you where
    you lie?

The good rain trickles down to you and laps your limbs about,
The young grass has its roots in you, your bones and members
    sprout.
Ah, poor untimely lover, in new fashion you'll discover
The clover still is fragrant, and the primroses are out.

Though the old uneasy feeling cannot wake you sleeping there,
Nor the soft spring breezes dally with your crisp delightful hair,
Yet the flowers are round you clinging, and the dust about you
    springing,
And your singing spirit wanders like an essence in the air.

John L. C. Brown

Casualty List

I

Will they never stop their chattering,
throwing misty drifts of words
over the bottomless pit
of their ignorance and my pain? . . .

I will go away.

I will be quiet for a little while,
and there will be no words to trouble the silence . . .

The jessamine in the silver vase is still,
each little starry face is still.

Only the firelight glows,
winks and shivers and glows again,
up and down the sides of the silver vase.

Like the red heart of pity . . .
The little jessamine faces

197

are sad,
thinking of . . .

I remember.

II

A number, a name, a place . . .

Perhaps he was asleep,
or else talking of Leontine
of Watou,
(missing his esses,
in that way he had,
queer and pleasant,
ever since a Turk bullet hit him in the mouth)
or singing rag-time with the other men,
when they got him.

Just some little trivial thing,
done every day,
and twenty times a day,
splashed suddenly with blood and dirt,
and so made the finale
of thirty ordinary years.

III

There is nothing in the quietness
save a dull ache
and a fury at the silliness of it all.

After all, his life was grey;
and even a splash of blood at the latter end
couldn't make death less grey.

There is only fury at the thought
of the obvious murderous silliness of his death,
the stupid mess of his life
in a dull circle of grey little pleasures,
and toil . . .

And I know
that HE, the innermost self of him,

was a thing to know and love.
A thing that all the greyness had not crushed
to its absolute likeness.

O! a man to love, a brother.

IV

But in six years or so? . . .

Dullness and dirtiness and toil
had finally made him their own . . .

How long, how long
shall there be something
that can grind the faces of poor men
to an ultimate uniformity of dullness
and grinning trivial meanness?

Or pitchfork them at will
(cheering and singing patriotic doggerel)
to a stinking hell,

to crash about for a little,
noisily, miserably;
till the inevitable comes,
and crushes them
bloodily, meanly?

V

The jessamine faces are very still,
waiting, waiting.

The fire gleams
up and down the side
of the cold silver vase,

angrily, like a fierce threat,
like a terrible rose
suddenly born out of the utter greyness of things.

Henry L. Simpson

The Grudge

'We grudged not those that were dearer than all we possessed,
Lovers, brothers, sons;
Our hearts were full, and out of a full heart
We gave our beloved ones.'

      The Bereaved, by Lawrence Binyon

We are of baser quality: we have been
Tried by fire and judged a spurious gold.
We are little of soul; and yet in our pigmy way
We have suffered and loved with a love that cannot be told.

Being less than you, we did not eagerly quaff
The cup of gall: we prayed that it might pass.
We are not gods; we are pitiful human stuff,
And the blood of our passion has stained Gethsemane's grass.

We were not blind to the vision. We heard the call
And followed, or watched our beloved steadfastly go.
But our grief is naked, and shivers, and will not be soothed
By splendid phrases, or clothed in a moral glow.

We cannot say for our comfort: "Losing them,
We gain a glimpse of noble, terrible heights,
A cleansing, exquisite pain, a sacred grief,
A dream to cherish"—we think of the vanished lights.

We think of the fine nerves shattered, the warm blood chilled,
The laughter silenced, the zest and beauty gone,
The desolation of wasted wonderful dreams
That will never be lived, of work that cannot be done.

1917

        Gerald Bullett

On a War-Worker, 1916

Far from their homes they lie, the men who fell
Fighting, in Flanders clay or Tigris sand:
She who lies here died for the cause as well,
Whom neither bayonet killed nor bursting shell,
But her own heart that loved its native land.

Arundell Esdaile

The Dead

Is it because that lad is dead
   My eyes are doing a double duty,
And drink, for his sake and in his stead,
   Twice their accustomed draught of beauty;

Or does the intoxicating Earth
   Ferment in me with stronger leaven,
Because, for seeing the year's rebirth,
   He loans me eyes that look on heaven?

Frank Sidgwick

The Halt

'Mark time in front! Rear fours cover! Company—halt!
Order arms! Stand at—ease! Stand easy.' A sudden hush:
   And then the talk began with a mighty rush—
'You weren't ever in step—The sergeant—It wasn't my fault—
Well, the Lord be praised at least for a ten minutes' halt.'
   We sat on a gate and watched them easing and shifting;
   Out of the distance a faint, keen breath came drifting,
From the sea behind the hills, and the hedges were salt.

Where do you halt now? Under what hedge do you lie?
   Where the tall poplars are fringing the white French roads/
And smoke I have not seen discolours the French sky?
Is the company resting there as we rested together,

Stamping its feet and readjusting its loads
And looking with wary eyes at the drooping weather?

Edward R. B. Shanks

To the Boys Lost in Our Cruisers

Others bring much, but these had most to bring;
   All hope, all dreams, life left an unrun race;
For that has death, the just and gentle king,
   Now set them first in place.

Sea-children! Still, by quiet copse and close,
   Safe through your service, other children play
Dear brothers are you now to all of those,
   For whom you died that day.

H.M.S. *Iron Duke*, 1914

Edward H. Young

Return

This was the way that, when the war was over,
We were to pass together. You, its lover,
Would make me love your land, you said, no less,
Its shining levels and their loneliness,
The reedy windings of the silent stream,
Your boyhood's playmate, and your childhood's dream.

The war is over now: and we can pass
This way together. Every blade of grass
Is you: you are the ripples on the river:
You are the breeze in which they leap and quiver.
I find you in the evening shadows falling
Athwart the fen, you in the wildfowl calling:
And all the immanent vision cannot save
My thoughts from wandering to your unknown grave.

St. Ives, 1919

Edward H. Young

Years Ahead

  Years ahead, years ahead,
    Who shall honour our sailor-dead?
For the wild North Sea, the bleak North Sea,
Threshes and seethes so endlessly.
Gathering foam and changing crest
Heave and hurry, and know no rest:
    How can they mark our sailor-dead
      In the years ahead?

  Time goes by, time goes by,
    And who shall tell where our soldiers lie?
The guiding trench winds cut afar,
Miles upon miles where the dead men are;
A cross of wood or a carven block,
A name-disc hung on a rifle-stock—
    These shall tell where our soldiers lie
      As the time goes by.

  Days to come, days to come—
    But who shall ask of the wandering foam,
The weaving weed, or the rocking swell,
The place of our sailor-dead to tell?
From Jutland reefs to Scapa Flow
Tracks of the wary warships go,
    But the deep sea-wastes lie green and dumb
      All the days to come.

  Years ahead, years ahead,
    The sea shall honour our sailor-dead!
No mound of mouldering earth shall show
The fighting place of the men below,
But a swirl of seas that gather and spill;
And the wind's wild chanty whistling shrill
    Shall cry, 'Consider my sailor-dead!'
      In the years ahead.

                                    Guy N. Pocock

Lament in 1915 (B.H.W.)

I call you, and I call you. Oh come home.
You lonely creature. Curse the foreign clown
Who plugged you with that lead, and knocked you down.
Stand up again and laugh, you wandering friend;
Say, as you would: 'It's just a little hole;
It will soon mend.'
Walk now into the room. Come! Come! Come! Come!

Come! We will laugh together all the night.
(We shall have poured ourselves a glass or two.)
Sit down. Our mutual mirth will reach its height
When we remember how they called you dead,
And I shall ask you how it felt, and you—
'Oh nothing. Just a tumble. Rather hot,
The feeling in my side; and then my head
A trifle dizzy, but I'm back again.
I lay out there too long, and I've still got,
When I think of it, just a little pain.'
I know the way you tumbled . . . Once you slid
And landed on your side. I noticed then
A trick of falling; not like other men.
But did your mouth drop open? Did your breath
Hurt you? What sort of feeling quickly came,
When you discovered that it might be death?

And what will happen if I shout your name?
Perhaps you may be there behind the door,
And if I raise my voice a little more,
You'll swing it open. I don't know how thick
The black partition is between us two.

Answer, if you can hear me; friend, be quick . . .
Listen, the door-bell rang! Perhaps it's you.
You're in the room. You're sitting in that chair.
You are! . . . I will go down. It *was* the bell.
You *may* be waiting at the door as well.

Am I not certain I shall find you there? . . .

You're rigged in your best uniform to-day;
You take a momentary martial stand,

204

Then step inside and hold me out your hand,
And laugh in that old solitary way.

You don't know why you did it. All this while
You've slaved and sweated. Now you're very strong,
And so you tell me with a knowing smile:
'We're going out to Flanders before long.'
I thought you would come back with an ugly hole below
    your thigh,
And ask for sympathy and wander lame;
I thought you'd be that same
Grumbling companion without self-control—
I never thought you'd die.

*   *   *

Now let us both forget this brief affair:
Let us begin our friendship all again.
I'm going down to meet you on the stair.
Walk to me! Come! For I can see you plain.
How strange! A moment I did think you dead.
How foolish of me!
Friend! Friend! Are you dumb?
Why are you pale? Why do you hang your head?
You see me? Here's my hand. Why don't you come?
Don't make me angry. You are there, I know.
Upstairs. You're tired. Lie down; you must come home.
And yet—Somehow it's dark down all the stair.
I'm standing at the door. You are not there.

Harold Monro

Elegy

(For J. N., died of wounds , October 1916)

So you are dead. We lived three months together,
    But in these years how absence can divide!
We did not meet again. I wonder whether
    You thought of me at all before you died.

There in that whirl of unaccustomed faces,
    Strange, friendless, ill, I found in you a friend
And then at last in these divided places
    You here in France, I here—and this the end.

For friendship's memory was short and faithless
    And time went by that would not come again,
And you are dead of wounds and I am scatheless
    Save as my heart has sorrowed for my slain.

I wonder whether you were long in dying,
    Where, in what trench, and under what dim star,
With drawn face on the clayey bottom lying,
    While still the untiring guns cried out afar.

I might have been with you, I might have seen you
    Reel to the shot with blank and staring eye,
I might have held you up . . . I might have been you
    And lain instead of you where now you lie.

Here in our quietude strange fancy presses,
    Dark thoughts of woe upon the empty brain,
And fills the streets and the unpleasant wildernesses
    With forms of death and ugly shapes of pain.

You are long dead. A year is nearly over,
    But still your voice leaps out again amid
The tangled memories that lie and cover
    With countless trails what then we said and did.

And still in waking dreams I sit and ponder
    Pleasures that were and, as my working brain
Deeper in revery will stray and wander,
    I think that I shall meet with you again

And make my plans and half arrange the meeting,
    And half think out the words that will be said
After the first brief, careless pleasant greeting . . .
    Then suddenly I remember you are dead.

                              Edward R. B. Shanks

The Last Meeting

III

I know that he is lost among the stars,
And may return no more but in their light.
Though his hushed voice may call me in the stir
Of whispering trees, I shall not understand.
Men may not speak with stillness; and the joy
Of brooks that leap and tumble down green hills
Is faster than their feet; and all their thoughts
Can win no meaning from the talk of birds.

My heart is fooled with fancies, being wise;
For fancy is the gleaming of wet flowers
When the hid sun looks forth with golden stare.
Thus, when I find new loveliness to praise,
And things long-known shine out in sudden grace,
Then will I think: 'He moves before me now.'
So he will never come but in delight,
And, as it was in life, his name shall be
Wonder awaking in a summer dawn,
And youth, that dying, touched my lips to song.

Flixécourt, May 1916

Siegfried Sassoon

In Memoriam F.

Thou art dead; there is no more
Of chatting by the open door,
Of theorising in the fields
Shaming the crops with wisdom's yields,
Or talking by the study fire
Planning jests and heart's desire.
Thou art dead; of these and thee
There is no more but memory.

Iolo A. Williams

Rupert Brooke

1887–1915

To have lived and loved—yea, even for a little,
　To have known the sun and fulness of the earth;
To have tested joy nor stayed to prove it brittle,
　And travelled grief to find it end in mirth;
To have loved the good in life, and followed, groping,
　Beauty that lives among the common things,
Awaiting, eager-eyed and strongly hoping,
　The faint far beating of an angel's wings.

All these were his. And with his soul's releasing,
　Dearest of all, immortal youth has crowned him,
　And that bright spirit is young eternally;
Dreaming, he hears the great winds blow unceasing,
　And over him, about him, and around him,
　The music and the thunder of the sea.

John L. C. Brown

In Memoriam S.C.W., V.C.

(8 September 1915)

There is no fitter end than this.
　No need is now to yearn nor sigh.
We know the glory that is his,
　A glory that can never die.

Surely we knew it long before,
　Knew all along that he was made
For a swift radiant morning, for
　A sacrificing swift night-shade.

Charles H. Sorley

When You See Millions of the Mouthless Dead

When you see millions of the mouthless dead
Across your dreams in pale battalions go,
Say not soft things as other men have said,
That you'll remember. For you need not so.
Give them not praise. For, deaf, how should they know
It is not curses heaped on each gashed head?
Nor tears. Their blind eyes see not your tears that flow.
Nor honour. It is easy to be dead.
Say only this, 'They are dead.' Then add thereto,
'Yet many a better one has died before.'
Then scanning all the o'ercrowded mass, should you
Perceive one face that loved hereuntofore,
It is a spook. None wears the face you knew.
Great death has made all his for evermore.

Charles H.Sorley

A Bitter Taste

Invitation au Festin

Oh come and live with me, my love,
    And share my war-time dinner.
Who eats the least at this our feast.
    Shall make John Bull the winner.

Here is a plate of cabbage soup,
    With caterpillars in.
How good they taste! (Avoid all waste,
    If you the war would win.)

Now, will you have a minnow, love,
    Or half an inch of eel?
A stickleback, a slice of jack,
    Shall grace our festive meal.

We've no unpatriotic joint,
    No sugar and no bread.
Eat nothing sweet, no rolls, no meat,
    The Food Controller said.

But would you like some sparrow pie,
    To counteract the eel?
A slice of swede is what you need,
    And please don't leave the peel.

But there's dessert for you, my love,
    Some glucose stewed with sloes.
And now good-night—your dreams be bright!
    (Perhaps they will,—who knows?)

Aelfrida Tillyard

The Survival of the Fittest
(In Memoriam, L.C. and T.)

'Those like Mr. Tomkins of *The* *****, who say that without war
the race would degenerate.'—*Star,* March 30, 1915.

These were my friends; Tomkins, you did not know them,
    For they were simple, unaspiring men;
No ordinary wind of chance could blow them
    Within the range of your austerest ken.
They were most uninformed. They never even—
    So ignorant and godless was their youth—
Heard you expound, with reverence to heaven,
    The elements of biologic truth.

Had they but had the privilege to cluster
    Around Gamaliel's feet, they would have known
That hate and massacre also have their lustre,
    And that man cannot live by Love alone.
But having no pillar of flame of your igniting
    To guide by night, no pillar of cloud by day,
They thought War was an evil thing, and fighting
    Filthy at best. So, thus deluded, they

Not seeing the war as a wise elimination
    Or a cleansing purge, or a wholesome exercise,
Went out with mingled loathing and elation
    Only because there towered before their eyes
England, an immemorial crusader,
    A great dream-statue, seated and serene,
Who had seen much blood, and sons who had betrayed her,
    But still shone out with hands and garments clean;

Summoning now with an imperious message
    To one last fight that Europe should be free,
Whom, though it meant a swift and bitter passage,
    They had to serve, for she served Liberty.

Romance and rhetoric! Yet with such nonsense nourished,
    They faced the guns and the dead and the rats and the rains,
And all in a month, as summer waned, they perished;
    And they had clear eyes, strong bodies, and some brains.

Tomkins, these died. What need is there to mention
 Anything more? What argument could give
A more conclusive proof of your contention?
 Tomkins, these died, and men like you still live.

J. C. Squire

Waste

Grub for gold with prisoned life;
Mint it at the price of breath;
Let it bear the stamp of strife;
Let it purchase power of death:
Life and gold, one wasted bar,
Lavish it on waste of war.

Dig the gold with good men's toil;
Leave the holes for dead men's graves;
Starve the growth, and hoard the spoil
Stored in trenches, heaped on waves:
Murder, lurking underground,
Till the trump of Azrael sound.

Drain the gold, and forge the chain;
Drain the strength, and bind the race;
Rouse the brute in man to reign;
Train him for his princely place:
Flunkey to a nation's pride
In the lust of fratricide.

Geoffrey W. Young

If I Should Die, be not Concerned to Know

If I should die, be not concerned to know
    The manner of my ending, if I fell
Leading a forlorn charge against the foe,
    Strangled by gas, or shattered by a shell.
Nor seek to see me in this death-in-life
    Mid shirks and curses, oaths and blood and sweat,
Cold in the darkness, on the edge of strife,
    Bored and afraid, irresolute, and wet.

But if you think of me, remember one
    Who loved good dinners, curious parody,
Swimming, and lying naked in the sun,
    Latin hexameters, and heraldry,
Athenian subtleties of δηζ and ποιζ,
    Beethoven, Botticelli, beer, and boys.

Philip Bainbrigge

If I Should Die . . .

If I should die just bury my flesh
In any hole that lets an angel through,
On any shore that loves a stormy sea,
Down any street that isn't paved with gold,
In any land where no one ever comes,
In any wilderness where flesh can hide,
On any mountain that will make amends
For all the sunsets I have never seen!

If I should die just bury my flesh
In any town of unassuming people,
In any land that makes an honest fuss,
In any box that's labelled with my name,
In any country waving any flag,
Or else in any cheering fatherland
That asks no loyalty of death but death!

If I should die just bury my flesh
In any forest that is full of leaves,

In any heaven that is full of shine,
In any shingle that is full of stars,
In any vineyard that is full of wrath,
In any firing-line my friends have filled
With long-dead lies that sent us to the fight!

Albert E. Tomlinson

The Strand 1917

Theatre time.
A corralling of colts, of steers and stallions, of youths in khaki
    and in chase of women; of women in little save the
    fragmentary, provocative dress of their trade.
And sprowling, Mediterranean-blue policemen to look after
    them.
Taxi-cabs, nettled because they are not permitted on the
    pavement to knock people over; to satisfy the blood-lust of
    swift machines.
Promiscuous strollers without collars or confidence, mingling
    more vicious, more expensive, syphilis-dodging sharks;
Well-to-do, assertive sharks in white shirt-fronts.

Hebrews everywhere, like blackheads on the face of man; of a
    man who has overlooked his nerves and blood into
    unhealthiness.
Hens of Jerusalem too, gathered under the wings of the
    transcontinental ponces' board.
Humans massing for rubbing of backs and souls together; for
    fear of balancing their odds in loneliness, and recalling in
    solitude the Ice which shall end Things.

A liquorous, lecherous pervadement of stench; body-stench with
    a frangipani dash.
Like a verdigrised, rancid slice of lemon in a beaker of very
    native-born firewater.
Small light, few lamps, and a little obscured laughter, because
    there is a War.
And it behoves robust patriots to remember the boys out There.

Midnight.
An unhealthy, devastating calm, where was unhealthy
    congestion.

And a discharging vehicular stench, surviving fitly the folk-
    stench;
A silence more unnaturally incestuously foul because of the
    furore that was.
And moonlight, in sluicing Augean travail to make Filth
    impossibly clean; to render adulteries pure.

There are some drunken drabs, and sailors, and reeling
    bowlegged men.
Unfits, indispensables, aliens and tipsy foreigners.

A shriek or so; a warm wave of tittering for the stomach's sake;
But patriotically subdued.
Colonials in camel-dung-coloured uniform with absurd hats.

The moon glares wildly on all, then giving up her job in a cloud
    of disgust,
Says, "Thank God, I am useful to guide a few big bombs to this
    opened drain."

Dawn.
Policemen and smells, and one or two adornments of fish-heads
    still linger; some medals of orange-peel, and ribbons from
    skinned bananas.
Soot-fungused walls, which once were white, grimace in the
    zinc-ointment light of the moon.
Disreputable heroes in stone gaze rather woebegonely blue
    about the eyelids, on the re-mobilising traffic.
A red mail-van rumbles and grumbles by.
A sort of bleached apologetic breeze tries to forbid the banns of
    daybreak and decay.
And very soon, the latest news of a week-old trench-raid is on
    the streets.
The casualty-list to follow.

Albert E. Tomlinson

A Hero

My father, when I went to war,
Grasped me with a pudgy paw,
"Good luck", he said, "My precious lad,
See you do credit to your Dad,
You're no age yet, you have the spunk,
I'd hate like Hell for you to funk.
If I could march I'd slope a gun
And help exterminate the Hun.
If my legs were twenty-five years younger
I'd ginger up the German Junger."

"Stout words, old Dad, perhaps you're right,
Pity you're too old to fight,
Pity you're not Peter Pan,
Your belly's like a beer-can;
There's backbone in your senile chatter,
As much as in a pot of batter."

"My boy, your simile's cheap and wooden,
Batter bakes us Yorkshire pudden,
And that's the stuff to give you guts,
And make you putt those ten-yard putts.
I'd try to 'list' as under forty
But the Bible says deceit is naughty.
Ah, would", he sighed, "this ghastly war
Had come but thirty years before."

"I'm with you here, I quite agree
That date would just have done for me
And incidentally done for thee."
"Your wits are keen, I once suspected
Your moral assets were neglected;
You intellectuals make me quiver,
You load the brain, but bleach the liver.
But now you've got a bloodhound's chance
To find your manhood out in France.
What finer finish to education
Than perishing for your pater's nation?
Go, and hold it no effrontery
To croak it for your king and country."

219

"Good-bye Dad, a thousand thanks
For giving me to swell the ranks;
Your magnanimity's no small dose,
You run old Abraham quite close;
God will requite our sacrifice
With expensive seats in paradise."

"Good-luck, my lad, should you perchance
Return a trifle soiled from France—
I'm despatching you upon approval,
So keep me primed with all the 'nouvelles'—
My welcome will be unreserved,
I'll shake such limbs as you've preserved
And find the job that you've deserved."

Off I went and saw the war
And thought it all a bloody bore;
I clawed and scratched for home and beauty,
And tramped some hundred miles for duty.
I cursed and dug and dropped a limb,
And leaked blood enough to dowse my glim.
My father almost wept an ocean,
But bore up, for I'd won promotion.

Discharged at length as no more use,
I felt like Portland broken loose;
I came back to a grateful land—
They tactlessly forgot the band—
My father seemed a bit put out
To see the hand I'd come without.
His welcome was at best reluctant,
Altruism's not a good inductant.

"I'll make allowance for your loss,
In spirit, not in filthy dross,
But times are bad, and living high,
The government's like a giblet pie.
You can't expect with one hand dud
To run a blasted racing stud.
Perhaps if I have any luck,
I'll find a job to suit your book."

He found it, deep down in a bank,
A concession to my captain's rank,
And now with sixty bob a week,
I lack a limb but got my keep.
Besides I've got a decoration;

I'm grateful to my pater's nation.

Albert E. Tomlinson
(Middlesbrough, January 1920)

Sed Miles

All the best
Have long gone West;
The East is cursed
With all the worst;
In this, at least,
Our Farthest East
Is London Port,
A sick resort
Where all the blood
Of Mametz Wood,
And all the guts
Of Mesnil Buttes,
And that slight Hell
At Poelcapelle,
Are suet and duff
For a journalist puff;
And the whole damn War
Little more
Than 'Latest News',
And 'Our Expert's Views'.

It's often said
You're a long time dead,
And the grey worms eat,
Through the nails of your feet,
Through the white of your thighs,
To the whites of your eyes;

You feel pretty cheap
As a drab little heap
Of powder and smell;
For a Fritz gas-shell
Leaves more behind
In the way of rind.

But when West you go
It's nice to know
You've done your bit
In spite of it;
And Blighty's name
And Blighty's fame
Will find in your
Demise, manure,
To sprout and spread
Till English red
Is the favourite hue
For Bartholomew,
And his maps all blush
With a porty flush,
And only Mars
And the minor stars
Are beyond the zone
Of the next War Loan;
When West you go
It's nice to know
You've done your bit
In spite of it.

Albert E. Tomlinson
(London, December 1916)

They

The Bishop tells us: "When the boys come back
They will not be the same; for they'll have fought
In a just cause; they lead the last attack
On Anti-Christ; their comrades' blood has bought
New right to breed an honourable race,
They have challenged Death and dared him face to face."

"We're none of us the same!" the boys reply.
"For George lost both legs; and Bill's stone blind;
Poor Jim's shot through the lungs and like to die;
And Bert's gone syphilitic; you'll not find
A chap who's served that hasn't found *some* change."
And the Bishop said: "The ways of God are strange!"

Siegfried Sassoon

Blighters

The House is crammed: tier beyond tier they grin
And cackle at the show, while prancing ranks
Of harlots shrill the chorus, drunk with din;
"We're sure the Kaiser loves our dear old Tanks!"

I'd like to see a Tank come down the stalls,
Lurching to rag-time tunes, or 'Home, sweet Home',
And there'd be no more jokes in Music-halls
To mock the riddled corpses round Bapaume.

Siegfried Sassoon

Base Details

If I were fierce and bald, and short of breath,
   I'd live with Scarlet Majors at the Base,
And speed glum heroes up the line to death.
   You'd see me with my puffy petulant face,
Guzzling and gulping at the best hotel,
Reading the Roll of Honour. 'Poor young chap',
I'd say—'I used to know his father well;
   Yes, we've lost heavily in this last scrap.'
And when the war is done and youth stone dead,
I'd toddle safely home and die—in bed.

Siegfried Sassoon

The General

"Good morning, good morning!" the General said
When we met him last week on our way to the line.
Now the soldiers he smiled at are most of 'em dead,
And we're cursing his staff for incompetent swine.
"He's a cheery old card", grunted Harry to Jack
As they slogged up to Arras with rifle and pack.

. . .

But he did for them both by his plan of attack.

Siegfried Sassoon

Does it Matter?

Does it matter?—losing your legs? . . .
For people will always be kind,
And you need not show that you mind
When the others come in after hunting
To gobble their muffins and eggs.

Does it matter?—losing your sight? . . .
There's such splendid work for the blind;
And people will always be kind,
As you sit on the terrace remembering
And turning your face from the light.

Do they matter?—those dreams from the pit? . . .
You can drink and forget and be glad,
And people won't say that you're mad;
For they'll know that you've fought for your country
And no one will worry a bit.

Siegfried Sassoon

Glory of Women

You love us when we're heroes, home on leave,
Or wounded in a mentionable place.
You worship decorations; you believe
That chivalry redeems the war's disgrace.
You make us shells. You listen with delight,
By tales of dirt and danger fondly thrilled.
You crown our distant ardours while we fight,
And mourn our laurelled memories when we're killed.
You can't believe that British troops 'retire'
When hell's last horror breaks them, and they run,
Trampling the terrible corpses—blind with blood.
   O German mother dreaming by the fire,
   While you are knitting socks to send your son
His face is trodden deeper in the mud.

Siegfried Sassoon

Suicide in the Trenches

I knew a simple soldier boy
Who grinned at life in empty joy,
Slept soundly through the lonesome dark,
And whistled early with the lark.

In winter trenches, cowed and glum,
With crumps and lice and lack of rum,
He put a bullet through his brain.
No one spoke of him again.

You smug-faced crowds with kindling eye
Who cheer when soldier lads march by,
Sneak home and pray you'll never know
The hell where youth and laughter go.

Siegfried Sassoon

O.B.E.

I know a Captain of Industry,
Who made big bombs for the R.F.C.,
And collared a lot of £ s. d.—
And he—thank God!—has the O.B.E.

I know a Lady of Pedigree,
Who asked some soldiers out to tea,
And said 'Dear me!' and 'yes, I see'—
And she—thank God!—has the O.B.E.

I know a fellow of twenty-three,
Who got a job with a fat M.P.—
(Not caring much for the Infantry.)
And he—thank God!—has the O.B.E.

I had a friend; a friend, and he
Just held the line for you and me,
And kept the Germans from the sea,
And died—without the O.B.E. Thank God!
He died without the O.B.E.

A. A. Milne

After the War

When the Last Long Trek is Over

When the last long trek is over,
   And the last long trench filled in,
I'll take a boat to Dover,
   Away from all the din;
I'll take a trip to Mendip,
   I'll see the Wiltshire downs,
And all my soul I'll then dip
   In peace no trouble drowns.

Away from noise of battle,
   Away from bombs and shells,
I'll lie where browse the cattle,
   Or pluck the purple bells;
I'll lie among the heather,
   And watch the distant plain,
Through all the summer weather,
   Nor go to fight again.

               Alec C. V. de Candole

Post Bellum

All things are mutable! The years recede,
And our vast shroud of smoke and flame must pass!
Another age with other eyes shall read
The moment's history; as thro' a glass,
It shall behold our striving and our toil,
Dissect the cause and calculate the gain.
Prating upon futility of wars,
Traverse for holiday the hallow'd soil
   Where now our slain
Lie, with their shatter'd faces to the stars.

Some there shall be, with restless hearts and bold,
Who, wrapp'd in ease, shall envy us the life
Of changing scenes and perils manifold,
Casting a gloss of glory on our strife.
But will no gleam last lambent thro' the years
Of squalor, pain, unending weariness,
Borne for a vision, dim descried but sure,
That by our agony and by our tears
   Concord shall bless
Our land, and they, our sons, shall dwell secure?

Geoffrey Fyson

A Farewell to Arms

'My helmet now shall make an hive for bees,' —Peele.

Now that the King has no more need of me
   I will devise a last farewell to arms,
And the great days of strength and chivalry,
   Of battles and excursions and alarms.
My helmet now shall hang above my bed,
   My pistol serve to scare birds from the grain,
And even my gas-mask stand by me in good stead
   Whenever I clean out the farmyard drain.

My lips, too, shall forget the soldier's curse
   And deal in comfortable words again;
And I will strive in my campaigns of verse
   To sing a song shall please my fellow men.

And Time, who has taken in trust my fighting days,
   Shall lead me through the land of Well-and-Fair,
Up hill and down, along the broad highway,
   Till the golden bowl breaks beyond all repair.

Digby B. Haseler

From 'To My Brother'

This I will do when peace shall come again—
Peace and return, to ease my heart of pain.
Crouched in the brittle reed-beds wrapped in grey
I'll watch the dawning of the winter's day,
The peaceful, clinging darkness of the night
That mingles with the mystic morning light,
And graceful rushes, melting in the haze,
While all around in winding waterways
The wildfowl gabble cheerfully and low,
Or wheel with pulsing whistle to and fro,
Filling the silent dawn with sweetest song,
Swelling and dying as they sweep along,
Till shadows of vague trees deceive the eyes
And stealthily the sun begins to rise,
Striving to smear with pink the frosted sky
And pierce the silver mist's opacity;
Until the hazy silhouettes grow clear
And faintest hints of colouring appear,
And the slow, throbbing, red, distorted sun
Reaches the sky, and all the large mists run,
Leaving the little ones to wreathe and shiver,
Pathetic, clinging to the friendly river;
Until the watchful heron, grim and gaunt,
Shows, ghostlike, standing at his favourite haunt,
And jerkily the moorhens venture out,
Spreading swift, circled ripples round about;
And softly to the ear, and leisurely
Querulous, comes the plaintive plover's cry.
And then, maybe, some whispering near by,
Some still small sound as of a happy sigh
Shall steal upon my senses, soft as air,
And, brother! I shall know that thou art there.

Then with my gun forgotten in my hand,
I'll wander through the snow-encrusted land,
Following the tracks of hare and stoat, and traces
Of bird and beast, as delicate as laces,
Doing again the things that we held dear,
Keeping thy gracious spirit ever near,
Comforted by the blissful certainty
And sweetness of thy splendid company.

And in the lazy summer nights I'll glide
Silently down the sleepy river's tide,
Listening to the music of the stream,
The plop of ponderously playful bream,
The water whispering around the boat,
And from afar the white owl's liquid note
That lingers through the stillness, soft and slow;
Watching the little yacht's red homely glow,
Her vague reflection, and her clean cut spars
Ink-black against the stillness of the stars,
Stealthily slipping into nothingness,
While on the river's moon-splashed surfaces
Tall shadows sweep. Then will I go to rest,
It may be that my slumbers will be blest
By the faint sound of thy untroubled breath,
Proving thy presence near, in spite of death.

Jeffery Day

Pin-Pricks

They were playing before a fireless grate . . .
When one of them suddenly pointed a fat finger
At the old Pear's Annual print, pasted on cardboard,
Now on its last legs and useful only
For stopping up a draught in the nursery chimney.

"Look, there are holes in it,
Tiny little holes all over the place."
"So there are! Look at these here in the pond!"
"And heaps and heaps on the road . . .
But none in the sky?"

Holes in it? What do you mean? . . . Where?
Let me see, my children. . . .

Ah God! How can I tell them,
Make them understand and feel, and pity the poor world?
That country scene was once the background,

The firm base into which we stuck the points. . . .
It all comes back to me now so vividly,
The buying of the map; the pins and flags
Stuck on them, stiffly sticking out so straight;
The excitement of moving them now and then,
The thrill of a slight advance,
Of a little bulge in the long line of pins;
The grief, heart-rending, shameful, of retreat,
As of the very stakes of God's claim uprooted. . . .
The wearying of it all after a while,
The silly monotony.
The drab, boring, continuous murder,
The ghastly stalemate so long, so long enduring. . . .

Stabbing steel and paper patriotism . . .
Each prick a hundred shell-holes and each flag
The token of a million high-held hearts
—Snared by a Press gang.
No use, then, kicking against the pricks. . . .
Insanity, loss of faith, bewilderment, despair,
Fear, agony, death and mutilation
—And all that a pin might shift by an eighth of an inch. . . .
Where are you now, stiff flags on piercing pins?
And where, O all you crushed hearts unfunctioning that
    hurt you when you laugh. . . .

"And none in the sky," you say?
That was "England" on our map, my children;
This village, these fields and woods that you love so well . . .
Look! It is still unscarred and smiling sweetly in the
    morning sunight!
But lives, hearts and souls were the price we paid
—Poured out into those pin-pricks carelessly,
Into the pond, and oh! . . . so thickly on the road—
That the sky might be clear . . . always . . . always. . . .

The village looks just ordinary, you think?
Go down on your knees, my children.
Screw up your little eyes.
Look deep and long into those holes,
And see (if you can) what Honour's dependence upon pain
Wrought in a dark pit, in a black Hell, blindly —

—That the village might look "just ordinary" this sweet
spring morning. . . .

Greville Cooke

On Passing the New Menin Gate

Who will remember, passing through this gate,
The unheroic Dead who fed the guns?
Who shall absolve the foulness of their fate,—
Those doomed, conscripted, unvictorious ones?
   Crudely renewed, the Salient holds its own.
   Paid are its dim defenders by this pomp;
   Paid, with a pile of peace-complacent stone,
   The armies who endured that sullen swamp.

Here was the world's worst wound. And here with pride
'Their name liveth for ever', the Gateway claims.
Was ever an immolation so belied
As these intolerably nameless names?
Well might the Dead who struggled in the slime
Rise and deride this sepulchre of crime.

Siegfried Sassoon

Biographical Notes

Martin Donisthorpe Armstrong (1882–1974)

He came up to Pembroke College from Charterhouse in 1902, and took his B.A. in Mechanical Engineering in 1905. He served in the ranks in the 2nd Artists' Rifles, 1914–15, and was commissioned in the 8th Middlesex Regiment, in which he served from 1915–19.

Philip Gillespie Bainbrigge (1890–1918)

He came up to Trinity College from Eton in 1909. He took his B.A. in Classics in 1912, and M.A. in 1916. From 1913 to March 1917 he taught at Shrewsbury School. In November 1917 he was commissioned in the 5th Battalion (Territorial) Lancashire Fusiliers, but was attached to the 15th Battalion Welsh Regiment from February 1918. While at Scarborough in February 1918 he made the acquaintance of Wilfred Owen. He was killed in action at Epehy on 18 September 1918.

Maurice Baring (1874–1945)

He came up to Trinity College from Eton in 1893. From 1897–1904 he was employed in the Diplomatic Service. He was foreign and war correspondent for the *Morning Post* in Manchuria, Russia, and Constantinople, and for *The Times* in the Balkans. As a Lieutenant in the 4th Hussars he took part in the Tirah Expedition, 1897–1898, and, from 1899–1900 in the South African War, in which he was severely wounded. From 1914–18 he served in the Intelligence Corps as Major and then Staff Officer. Later he transferred to the Royal Flying Corps. In 1918 he was made Hon. Wing Commander, R.A.F. He was mentioned in despatches, was awarded the O.B.E. in 1919, and became Chevalier, Légion d'Honneur in 1935.

Robert Harold Beckh (1894–1916)

He came up to Jesus College from Haileybury in 1913. After enlisting as a private in the Royal Fusiliers (Public Schools Battalion) he was commissioned in the East Yorkshire Regiment. He had planned to work as a clergyman in India after the war. From March 1916 he served in France, and on 15 August 1916 was killed by German machine-gun fire while out on patrol. He is buried in Cabaret-Rouge Cemetery, Souchez.

Ferenc Békássy (1893–1915)

He came up to King's College from Bedales in 1911, and took his B.A. in History in 1914. His parents belonged to the landed aristocracy in Hungary, and sent him and his five brothers and sisters in turn to receive the unconventional Bedalian education which included country pursuits. At King's he quickly made friends with Maynard Keynes (who visited him in Hungary in the summer of 1913), and became a member of the exclusive debating society, the Apostles. When war broke out he was anxious to return home to fight for the Austro-Hungarian Empire. Keynes helped him avoid internment and also gave him financial assistance for the journey back to Hungary. Békássy enlisted in the cavalry, and four days after arriving at the front was killed in action against the Russians at Dobrovouc in Bukovina. Keynes was also responsible for the memorial plaque to Békássy in King's College Chapel. His published work includes verse written in Hungarian and English (the latter published by the Hogarth Press in 1925).

Stuart Bellhouse (1894–1926)

He came up to Emmanuel College from Ilkley Grammar School in 1913. He enlisted in the West Riding (Howitzer) Brigade in 1914, and was soon commissioned in the 8th Battalion West Yorkshire Regiment (Leeds Rifles). He was wounded in 1915 and badly gassed in 1917. After the war he returned to Cambridge and took his B.A. in English in 1920. After a spell of journalism in Ireland he worked for a London press agency. However, his lungs had been permanently damaged by gas in the war and he died suddenly from heart failure in 1926.

Frederic William Bendall (1882–1953)

He came up to Selwyn College from Ipswich School in 1901. He took his B.A. in Classics in 1904. He then taught in Horsham and Bridlington. He served with the Territorial Force from 1910 in the 3rd Battalion (Royal Fusiliers), London Regiment. He was promoted to Lieutenant-Colonel in 1914 and served in Malta, the Sudan, Gallipoli, and France. In 1917 he was twice mentioned in despatches, and in 1918 was made C.M.G. In 1920 he was appointed H.M. Inspector for Secondary Schools. He served as the Director for Army Education, 1940–1942.

Rupert Chawner Brooke (1887–1915)

He came up to King's College from Rugby in 1906 to read Classics. He was linked with the Georgian movement in poetry, and moved in Fabian circles. His striking physical presence and personal charm affected all those who met him. Before the war he traveled in Germany, America, and the South Seas. He enlisted in 1914 as a Sub-Lieutenant in the Royal Naval Division. He died of septicaemia on his way to Gallipoli with the Hood Battalion. He was buried in an isolated grave on the island of Skyros. Immediately after his death an extravagant mythologizing process gathered momentum. His *1914 and Other Poems*, published in 1915, went through numerous reprintings, and was still widely purchased and read during and after the Second World War.

John Lewis Crommelin-Brown (1888–1953)

He came up to Trinity College from Westminster in 1907. He took his B.A. in Natural Sciences in 1910, and M.A. in 1922. He was commissioned in the Royal Garrison Artillery in 1915. He served in France from February 1916, but was invalided back to England with shell shock a month later. From May 1917 to July 1918 he was an instructor at the Cadet School, Trowbridge. He was promoted Lieutenant in 1917, and served in Salonika from August 1918 to May 1918. He was demobilized in June 1919 with the rank of Captain.

Gerald William Bullett (1893–1958)

Born in South London, he left the Stationers' School at the age of sixteen to work in a bank. He served with the Royal Flying

Corps in France. His first novel, *The Progress of Kay*, was published in 1916 while he was on active service in France. After the war, with an ex-serviceman's grant for further education, and with the support of Sir Arthur Quiller-Couch (whom he had never met, but to whom he had sent a copy of his novel, together with a request to help him secure a place at Cambridge), he came up to Jesus College in 1919, eventually taking his B.A. in English (1st class with Distinction). He was a writer for the rest of his life: novelist, short-story writer, biographer, poet, and anthologist.

Margaret Isabel Postgate Cole (1893–1980)

She was born in Cambridge, and came up to Girton College from Roedean in 1911. She took her B.A. (1st class) in Classics in 1914. In 1918 she married G. D. H. Cole, a leading Fabian. She wrote, lectured, and worked assiduously on behalf of the Labour Party and the Fabians. Her wide range of writing includes a series of twenty-nine detective novels written jointly with her husband. She was made a D.B.E. in 1970.

Greville Cooke (1894–1982)

Born in London, he was educated at Hamilton House, Ealing, the Royal Academy of Music, and Christ's College. He studied Theology at Ridley Hall, Cambridge, and was ordained in 1918. After various church appointments he became Canon of Peterborough Cathedral. From 1925–59 he was Professor at the Royal Academy of Music. He wrote books on religious and musical topics, as well as two volumes of poetry.

Robert Offley Ashburton Crewe-Milnes (Marquess of Crewe) (1858–1945)

He came up to Trinity College from Harrow in 1875. He took his B.A. in 1880, and M.A. in 1885. He worked in the following capacities: Assistant Private Secretary to the Foreign Secretary, 1883–84; Lord in Waiting to the Queen, 1886; Lord Lieutenant of Ireland, 1892–95; Lord President of the Council, 1905–08 and 1915–16; Lord Privy Seal, 1908 and 1912–15; Secretary of State for the Colonies, 1908–10; Secretary of State for India, 1910–15; President, Board of Education, 1916. When Asquith's Coalition fell he declined to take office under Lloyd George, and led the

Independent Liberal Opposition in the Lords. Later posts included: Chairman, L.C.C., 1917; H.M. Ambassador, Paris, 1922–1928; Secretary of State for War, 1931.

Miles Jeffery Game Day (1896–1918)

He was educated at Repton, and had been accepted at St. John's College, although he was never able to take up his place at the college. He enlisted in the Royal Naval Air Service at the start of the war, and served as a pilot with the rank of Flight Commander. He was killed on 27 February 1918 when his plane was shot down in air combat, and was awarded a posthumous D.S.C. His name appears on a memorial tablet in the college, and, since he has no known grave, on Panel 30 of the Chatham Naval Memorial.

Alec Corry Vully De Candole (1897–1918)

He was educated at Marlborough, where he was a younger contemporary of Charles Sorley, and won an Open Classical Exhibition to Trinity College. He was admitted to the college in October 1916, but did not sign the admissions book or matriculate. He was commissioned in the 4th Battalion Wiltshire Regiment, and was sent to Flanders in April 1917. In October 1917 he was wounded and invalided home. He returned to Belgium in July 1918. At the beginning of September 1918 the battalion was at Aubigny, near Arras, and on 4 September he was killed while taking part in a bombing raid at Boningues. He is buried in Aubigny Communal Cemetery Extension.

Arundell James Kennedy Esdaile (1897–1978)

He came up to Magdalene College from Lancing in 1899. He took his B.A. in 1902, and M.A. in 1924. He worked for ten years in the British Museum Library. He wrote four collections of verse, but most of his published work is in the fields of librarianship and bibliography.

William Norman Ewer (1885–1976)

He took his B.A. at Trinity College in 1907. After the war he worked as a socialist journalist, and was foreign editor of the Herald in 1919.

Geoffrey Fyson (1892–1948)

After leaving King Edward's School, Bath, he was employed in the National Provincial Bank, Cheltenham, while at the same time working as a freelance journalist. In 1914 he joined the Sportsman's Battalion as a private. He was wounded in France, and later commissioned in the Devonshire Regiment. In 1917 he was gassed. He entered Fitzwilliam House in 1918, obtaining first a Diploma in Forestry and a Degree in Economics. After a short spell in the Civil Service he returned to Cambridge to take the Education Diploma. From 1923–1927 he was Director of Education for the Scilly Isles. He then taught in Hendon until 1932. When his father died in 1932 he became managing director of Fyson's printing firm in Bath. He wrote poetry, criticism, and articles for many publications.

Ada May Harrison (1899–1958)

She was born in South Africa, and came up to Newnham College from St. Paul's Girls' School in 1918. She took her B.A. in Italian in 1921. In 1924 she married Professor R. S. Austin. Apart from short spells of teaching and social work she wrote a number of books about Italy, five children's books, as well as contributions to various newspapers and periodicals. She also broadcast on the BBC's "Woman's Hour."

Digby Bertram Haseler (1897–1978)

After leaving Hereford Cathedral School in 1916 he gained a place at St. John's College which he did not take up immediately. Instead, he enlisted in the King's Shropshire Light Infantry, and served with them until 1918. He eventually came up to St. John's in 1919, and took his B.A. in History in 1922. The son of a rector, he too was destined for the Church, working first in Cawnpore, then Hackney, Shropshire, Essex, and Yorkshire. His poem, "At a British Cemetery in Flanders," first appeared in the college magazine, the *Eagle*.

Henry Head (1861–1940)

He came up to Trinity College from Charterhouse in 1880. He took his B.A. (1st Class Natural Sciences) in 1884, and M.A. in 1888. He was made Hon. Fellow in 1920. He became a distinguished physician, and did pioneering work in the field of neurology. From 1914–19 he gave up his private practice at London Hospital and lived at the hospital devoting his whole time to treating the numerous wounded soldiers who were patients there. He was knighted in 1927. Most of his published work was in the field of medicine. He died, ironically, from Parkinson's disease, on which he was considered a leading authority.

Florence Edgar Hobson (?-?)

No biographical details available (she was not a student at either Girton College or Newnham College).

Alfred Edward Housman (1859–1936)

He was educated at Bromsgrove School before going up to St. John's College, Oxford, to study Classics. From 1882–92 he was the Professor of Latin at University College, London. From 1892–1911 he worked at the Patents Office. His celebrated poem, "A Shropshire Lad," was published in 1896. He was a Fellow of Trinity College from 1911 to 1936.

Thomas Edward Hulme (1883–1917)

He came up to St. John's College from the High School, Newcastle-under-Lyme on a Mathematics Exhibition, but was sent down in 1904 for disciplinary shortcomings. After some time abroad he returned to London and became involved in the birth of the Imagist movement in poetry. In London he mixed with the leading figures of the avant-garde, such as Wyndham Lewis, Henri Gaudier-Brzeska, and Ezra Pound. He returned to St. John's briefly in 1912, but soon left to study philosophy in Berlin. When the war started he enlisted in the Honourable Artillery Company. He was in Flanders from January to April 1915. An arm wound meant he was invalided back to England. While in England he became involved in a polemic with Bertrand Russell. Articles and letters by both men appeared in the *Cambridge Magazine* during the early months of 1916. In March 1916 Hulme was commissioned in the Royal Marine Artillery, and served in Belgium. He returned to England on leave in August 1917. Soon after going back to Belgium he was killed near Nieuport by a shell on 8 September 1917. His literary output on the war consists of a handful of poems, the above-mentioned articles, and his war diary. He is buried in Coxyde Military Cemetery, plot 4, row C, grave 2.

Donald Frederick Goold Johnson (1890–1916)

He came up to Emmanuel College from Caterham School in 1911. He took his B.A. in 1914 (Part I History, Part II Modern Languages). In 1914 he was awarded the Chancellor's Medal for English Verse for a poem on the Southern Pole. He was commissioned in the 2nd Battalion Manchester Regiment in February 1915. He went out to France at the end of 1915, and was killed while leading an attack on 15 July 1916. He is buried in Bouzincourt Communal Cemetery Extension.

Rose Macaulay (1889–1958)

Her father, G. C. Macaulay, was a Lecturer in English at Cambridge, and her uncle, W. H. Macaulay, was Senior Tutor at King's College. During the war, while living at Great Shelford, near Cambridge, she contributed to the home-front effort by working as a V.A.D. nurse at a military convalescent home on the Gog Magog hills, and as a land-girl on Station Farm. Throughout her distinguished literary career she won critical acclaim and prestigious literary awards (e.g., the Femina Vie Heureuse prize for *Dangerous Ages* in 1921, and the James Tait memorial prize for *The Towers of Trebizond* in 1956). Further honors came her way: Hon. D. Litt., Cambridge, in 1951, and D.B.E. in 1958.

John D. Macleod (?-?)

He was a student at Corpus Christi College. He served as a Captain with the Cameron Highlanders, and also with the Machine Gun Corps.

Alan Alexander Milne (1882–1956)

He came up to Trinity College from Westminster in 1900. In 1902 he was editor of *Granta*. He took his B.A. in 1903. From 1906 to 1914 he was Assistant Editor of *Punch* magazine. He was commissioned in the Royal Warwickshire Regiment and served with them from 1915 to 1918. After being wounded he was employed at the War Office. Although he wrote a number of plays he is best known for his children's classics, *Winnie the Pooh*, *The House at Pooh Corner*, *When We Were Very Young*, and *Now We Are Six*.

Harold Monro (1879–1932)

He came up to Gonville & Caius College from Radley in 1898. He took his B.A. in Medieval and Modern Languages in 1901. He was commissioned in the Royal Garrison Artillery, serving in an antiaircraft battery. He was later transferred to the War Office. He founded the influential *Poetry Review* in 1912, and in 1913 started the Poetry Bookshop, an institution that he ran until his death. With these two ventures he made a significant contribution to English literary life. He edited various anthologies of poetry as well as writing and publishing his own verse.

John Arnold Nicklin (1871–1917)

He came up to St. John's College from Shrewsbury and took his B.A. (1st in Classics) in 1894. He worked as a teacher as well as writing for the *Daily Chronicle* and *Tribune*. It seems he did no military service. His published work consists of verse and translations.

Oswald Norman (1863–1936)

He came up to Emmanuel College in 1880. He took his B.A. in 1884, M.A. in 1888, and LL.M. in 1891. He was called to the Bar in 1892, and awarded LL.D. in 1900.

Barry Pain (?-1928)

He came up to Corpus Christi College from Sedbergh. During the war he served as Chief Petty Officer in the Royal Naval Volunteer Reserve from 1915–16, and later, on the London Appeal Tribunal. He contributed to *Granta*, and besides poetry wrote novels and short stories.

Vivian Telfer Pemberton (1894–1918)

He came up to Sidney Sussex College from Cheltenham. There was only time to take Part I of the Mathematics Tripos before he was commissioned in the Royal Munster Fusiliers in 1914. In

243

1915 he was transferred to the Royal Garrison Artillery, and later promoted to Major. He was awarded the M.C. in 1918, and was killed in action on 7 October 1918 at Bellicourt. He is buried in Bellicourt British Cemetery.

Guy Noel Pocock (1880–1955)

He came up to St. John's College from Highgate School. He took his B.A. in 1904. He taught at Cheltenham College and at the Royal Naval College, Dartmouth. He later worked for the BBC. His literary output included novels, essays, anthologies, and books on the teaching of English.

Alfred Victor Ratcliffe (1887–1916)

He came up to Sidney Sussex College from Dulwich in 1907, and took his B.A. in 1914. He enlisted at the outbreak of the war, abandoning his studies to become a barrister at the Inner Temple. He was commissioned in the 10th Battalion West Yorkshire Regiment, and was killed, leading his company into action, on 1 July 1916, the opening day of the Battle of the Somme. He is buried in Fricourt New Military Cemetery which is situated in the middle of that part of No Man's Land which the West Yorkshires attempted to cross in the morning attack. In it are the graves of 159 men of the 10th Battalion West Yorkshire Regiment. No other battalion suffered such severe losses during that fateful day.

Siegfried Loraine Sassoon (1886–1967)

He came up to Clare College from Marlborough in 1905 to read Law, but soon switched to History. However, he derived no more satisfaction or success in this discipline and decided to leave Cambridge after just four terms in 1907. In August 1914 he enlisted as a trooper in the Sussex Yeomanry. In May 1915 he was commissioned in the 3rd Battalion Royal Welch Fusiliers. In November 1915 he was attached to the 1st Battalion in France where he met Robert Graves. Sassoon was an exceptionally brave (some would say unnecessarily reckless) soldier. His nickname, "Mad Jack," was not undeserved. He was awarded the M.C. in June 1916. In April 1917 he was wounded in the shoulder and was invalided home with trench fever. His disillusionment with the war led him to throw away his M.C. ribbon, and in July 1917 he issued a statement protesting against the politicians and on behalf of the suffering soldiery (see Appendix B). This was read out in the House of Commons and reported in *The Times*. He was sent to Craiglockhart psychiatric hospital to be treated for shell shock. Here he met Wilfred Owen. His later war poems, with their satirical punch and passionate antiwar views, are generally rated more highly than the early ones. In 1916 a number of his poems appeared in the *Cambridge Magazine*. He went back to France, received a head wound in July 1918 and was invalided home again. He was demobilized in March 1919 with the rank of Captain. Between 1928 and 1936 he wrote his trilogy of autobiographical war novels, *Memoirs of a Fox-Hunting Man*, *Memoirs of an Infantry Officer*, and *Sherston's Progress*. His autobiographical *Siegfried's Journey* appeared in 1945. He was awarded the C.B.E. in 1951.

Kenneth James Saunders (1883–1937)

He came up to Emmanuel College in 1902, taking his B.A. in Natural Sciences and Medicine in 1905. He followed this with a 1st in Theology in 1907, and M.A. in 1915. He was readmitted to the College in 1924. In 1925 he was awarded Lit. D.

Owen Seaman (1861–1936)

He came up to Clare College from Shrewsbury, and took his B.A. (1st class in Classics) in 1883. He joined the staff of *Punch* magazine in 1897 and was editor from 1906–32. He was knighted in 1914. His war poems, a mixture of light and serious, appeared in *Punch* and three volumes of verse.

Edward Buxton Shanks (1892–1953)

He came up to Trinity College from Merchant Taylors' in 1910, and took his B.A. in History in 1913. He was editor of *Granta* from 1912–13. After enlisting in the Artists' Rifles in August 1914 he was commissioned in December 1914 in the 8th Battalion South Lancashire Regiment. In April 1915 he was invalided out and worked in the War Office for the remainder of the war. In 1919 he was the first recipient of the Hawthornden Prize. After the war he was linked with the Georgian movement in poetry. He was Lecturer in Poetry at Liverpool University in

1926, and, from 1928–35, chief leader-writer for the *Evening Standard*.

Fredegond Shove (née Maitland) (1889–1949)

Her father was Downing Professor of Laws of England at Cambridge. She received private tuition before coming up to Newnham College in 1910. She read English but left without sitting the Tripos in 1913. She married Gerald Shove, Fellow of King's College. Her published work includes poetry, a memoir, and, in 1931, a study of Christina Rossetti.

Frank Sidgwick (?-?)

He was a student at Trinity College and took his B.A. in 1901. He served in the army. He was half of the publishing firm, Sidgwick & Jackson, which was responsible for publishing many slim volumes of poetry during and immediately after the war, including some of the poets represented in this anthology, e.g., Rupert Brooke, Jeffery Day, Rose Macaulay, John Nicklin, Edward Shanks, Frank Sidgwick, and E. Hilton Young.

Henry Lamont Simpson (1897–1918)

He was educated at Carlisle Grammar School, was accepted for admission to Pembroke College, but was killed at Hazebrouck on 29 August 1918. He had been commissioned in the 1st Battalion Lancashire Fusiliers in June 1917. His name is recorded on the Vis-en-Artois Memorial to the Missing at Haucourt.

Charles Hamilton Sorley (1895–1915)

He was a pupil at King's College School from 1906–8. His father was Professor of Moral Philosophy at Cambridge. He was killed on 13 October 1915, a Captain in the 7th Battalion Suffolk Regiment. He has no known grave and is commemorated on Panels 37 and 38 of the Loos Memorial. His early death cut short what many believe would have been a brilliant academic and/or literary career. The small amount of poetry he managed to write, together with his letters, reveal a young man of exceptional artistic promise, with a finely tuned critical intelligence (see Appendix A).

John Collings Squire (1884–1958)

He came up to St. John's College from Blundell's. He was deemed unfit for active service because of poor eyesight. He was one of the Georgian group of poets. He worked on the *New Statesman*, and edited the *London Mercury* from 1919–1934. Apart from his own work he published many anthologies and editions of the work of other poets. He was knighted in 1933.

Aelfrida Tillyard (1883-?)

She was born in Cambridge, and was educated in Lausanne, and at the University of Florence. Her brother, the Shakespearean scholar, E. M. W. Tillyard, became Master of Jesus College. She donated the profits from the sale of her volume of verse, *The Garden and the Fire*, to the Serbian Relief Fund.

Albert Ernest Tomlinson (1892–1968)

He came up to Emmanuel College from Middlesbrough High School in 1912. He took his B.A. in Modern Languages in 1914, and M.A. in 1919. He enlisted in the South Staffordshire Regiment on 4 June 1915, and had two spells in France, from March to July 1916, and from August 1917 to January 1918. He had been wounded in July 1916 and spent most of the following year recuperating in England and working for the War Office. On 25 September 1918 he was posted to India, arriving there on 3 November 1918. He was finally demobilized in 1919. Much of his verse is regional: Yorkshire, and, in later years, Suffolk, supplied his subject matter. With unrestrained northern bluntness he gave full vent to his antipathy toward the fawning admirers around Brooke, as well as toward Brooke himself, in a diatribe (unpublished) of vitriolic intensity (see Appendix C).

Kathleen Montgomery Wallace (née Coates) (1890-?)

She was born in Cambridge. Her father, William Montgomery Coates, was Bursar and Assistant Tutor at Queens' College. She came up to Girton College from the Perse High School, Cambridge, in 1909. A year's absence through illness meant she did not take her B.A. in English until 1914. Her brother, Basil Montgomery Coates, came up to Queens' College in 1912. He was killed in action on 7 September 1915. His death is mourned in a number of her elegiac poems, and his name appears on the Memorial Board in the College Chapel. She married Major J. H. Wallace in 1917. She wrote a number of novels and was a regular contributor to many women's magazines.

Iolo Aneurin Williams (1890–1962)

He came up to King's College from Rugby in 1910. He took his B.A. in History and Modern Languages in 1914. He was commissioned in the Yorkshire Regiment (T.F.) and later served on the General Staff. His published work includes poetry and bibliography. He was a regular contributor to a number of newspapers. His wide interests included botany and Welsh affairs (he spoke and wrote Welsh fluently).

Edward Hilton Young (1879–1960)

He was the younger brother of Geoffrey Winthrop Young (see below) and came up to Trinity College from Eton in 1897. He took his B.A. in Natural Sciences (1st class) in 1900, and M.A. in 1906. He was President of the Union in 1900. He was called to the Bar, Inner Temple in 1904. He was commissioned in 1914 and served as Lieutenant-Commander in the Royal Naval Volunteer Reserve, and was awarded the D.S.C. in 1915. He served at Archangel and in 1918 lost an arm at Zeebrugge. He was awarded the D.S.O. in 1919. From 1915–35 he served as Member of Parliament. In 1922 he married the sculptress, Katharine Scott, the widow of Captain Robert Falcon Scott. He was Minister of Health, 1931–35, and was created First Baron Kennet in 1935.

Geoffrey Winthrop Young (1876–1958)

He was the elder brother of Edward Hilton Young (see above). He came up to Trinity College from Marlborough in 1895, and took his B.A. in 1898, and M.A. in 1902. He was awarded the Chancellor's Medal for English Verse in 1898 and again in 1899. He taught at Eton from 1900–1905, and was H.M. Inspector for Schools from 1905–13. During the war he commanded Red Cross ambulance units in France, Belgium, and Italy. After being wounded he had a leg amputated. In spite of this handicap he was a leading British mountaineer. Apart from *The Roof Climber's Guide to Trinity* he wrote a number of more orthodox mountaineering books. From 1932–41 he was Reader in Comparative Education at London University. He was President of the Alpine Club from 1941–44.

Appendix A

THE FOLLOWING EXTRACT IS PART OF A LETTER DATED 28 APRIL 1915.
While Charles Sorley was at Aldershot he wrote to his mother
after hearing of the death of Rupert Brooke. The letter contains
a concise and perceptive analysis of Brooke's *1914* sonnets that
underlines the major differences between the outlook of each
man. Sorley rejects the Big Abstractions and the Grand Ges-
tures:

> That last sonnet sequence of his, of which you sent me the review in
> the *Times Literary Supplement*, and which has been so praised, I
> find (with the exception of that beginning 'Their hearts were woven
> of human joys and cares . . .' which is not about himself) overpraised.
> He is far too obsessed with his own sacrifice regarding the going to
> war of himself (and others) as a highly intense, remarkable and sac-
> rificial exploit, whereas it is merely the conduct demanded of him
> (and others) by the turn of circumstances, where the non-compliance
> with this demand would have made life intolerable. It was not that
> 'they' gave up anything of that list he gives in one sonnet: but that
> the essence of these had been endangered by circumstances over
> which he had no control and he must fight to recapture them. He has
> clothed his attitude in fine words: but he has taken the sentimental
> attitude.

Appendix B

WHILE RECOVERING FROM HIS WOUNDS AT HOME IN ENGLAND IN the summer of 1917 Siegfried Sassoon felt it was necessary to issue a form of protest in addition to his poetry. Philip and Lady Ottoline Morrell urged him to work with Bertrand Russell and Middleton Murry so as to produce a statement of protest. Copies were printed and distributed to influential people and to the press. On 31 July it appeared in *The Times*. Sassoon knew full well what he was doing and expected a court-martial. Friends such as Robert Graves were horrified and disapproving. He avoided court-martial and was sent to Craiglockhart War Hospital, near Edinburgh, where officers were treated for shell shock. While there he made the acquaintance of Wilfred Owen (Wilson 1998, 351–86). This was Sassoon's statement of protest:

> I am making this statement as an act of wilful defiance of military authority, because I believe that the War is being deliberately prolonged by those who have the power to end it. I am a soldier, convinced that I am acting on behalf of soldiers. I believe that the War, upon which I entered as a war of defence and liberation, has now become a war of aggression and conquest. I believe that the purposes for which I and my fellow-soldiers entered upon this War should have been so clearly stated as to have made it impossible for them to be changed without our knowledge, and that, had this been done, the objects which actuated us would now be attainable by negotiation.
>
> I have seen and endured the sufferings of the troops, and I can no longer be a party to prolonging those sufferings for ends which I believe to be evil, and unjust.
>
> I am not protesting against the military conduct of the War, but against the political errors and insincerities for which the fighting men are now being sacrificed.
>
> On behalf of those who are suffering now, I make this protest against the deception which is being practised on them. Also I believe that it may help to destroy the callous complacence with which the majority of those at home regard the continuance of agonies which they do not share, and which they have not sufficient imagination to realise.

Appendix C

THE FOLLOWING EXTRACTS ARE TAKEN FROM AN UNDATED TWENTY-five-page typescript (in the Tomlinson papers held in the archives of Emmanuel College) by Albert Ernest Tomlinson entitled "Rupert Brooke":

I did not fall dead at his feet when I met Rupert Brooke. I didn't even put 'Nunc Dimittis' on the gramophone. Sure enough, his countenance was as the sun, ruddy and comely withal, but [in] other ways he was not more than ordinary sacramental. He had a masculine *vox humana* and a large ration of freestone hair, but no two-edged swords, or even seven stars, or other supernal gear. The sum of his obituary sob-stuff is colossal enough to give the public myopia and him wings [. . . .]

He had a sweet smile. He was doing a dissertation on Russian plays to a crazy club at Cambridge—the Heretics, whatsoever they may be, something to eat possibly.[1] His facial outfit should have recalled Apollo, Romeo, Cléo de Mérode, and Praxiteles' celebrated sculp[ture] of Mercutio [*sic*], but I have no SOUL. I was thankful to be not more than bearably bored. I thought he had almost a squint.

His audience was fine, full, rich and grapy, with assorted Feminines. The room was medium, nondescript roomy room just over a fish-shop. His articulation, however, was so transcendental that every syllable was superlatively audible in spite of the turbot. Sleep was not possible. The young ladies hitched their esoteric suspenders to every comma in mesmerised coma. They have had their revenge since, in feverish frolics. Perhaps they were doing an autopsy in sonnet form even then.

Those hypnotised virgins didn't seem to get his goat. He ran his artistic talons through his coiffure and smiled absorbedly, as though to say, "I know I am leonine and irresistible, my dears, but not more divine than devilish. I missed being Adonis by three thousand years, so don't you get living deliciously on my account. If you must be enthralled, do be aloof. If you can't be good, do be gentlemen." [. . . .] When he touched on the drama that costs you half-a-crown in the pit these days the Girton harem giggled satanically. I knew I was bunched against the most Skyscraping Thought. [. . . .] The adoration in the rapt eyeballs of those damsels made me damn the hearty feed I'd done at dinner [. . . .]

When he had finished perpetrating the paper his palpitating audience leapt into the discussion with naked teeth. He dismissed whole choiring quires of queries with the air of a stipendiary magistrate at the Apocalypse. What he said, went: we all felt that and so did he. He blew his nose with a white handkerchief every so often—trivial detail, but how human! Any one of those Minervas would have rent her best georgette camisole to have done so much. [. . . .] I simply smelt that everyone was ignoring me to the very vertices of their ivory appalling right-angled shoulders [. . . .]

So there it is. Rupert's permanent address, Lake Superior, sublimely superior if you like, but superior. Rare character, fine bouquet, full blooded, great vinosity, generous yet delicate, very superior Cuvée. In other respects he seemed a likeable lad [. . . .] he had such soulful optics that he slipped into a pose as slickly as an actor into a bar, or a comedy chorus into pyjamas. All those hypercultivated Eves of Newnham did it [. . . .]

He lived poetry instead of living life, and he wrote Academic Abstraction [. . . .] His vapours are pervaded with all the old pedantic Hellenic perfumes—love, landscape, truth, death, duty and shining things—he merely does a new analysis with prismatic effects and a duplex lens [. . . .]

He was born with the Public School affliction. Others catch it along with the English Stare about the age of twelve, but Rupert had the growth from birth. His father was House-Master at Rugby. They make locomotives and mechanic electric modern things at Rugby too, but Rupert was diligently winning Waterloo with his patrician stable-mates, and never worried about chimneys and triple-expansion eight-cylinder trifles of the twentieth century [. . . .]

[. . . .] the cheerful prose of his *Letters from America* are the most vivid virile poetry he ever evolved. Read them and rejoice. I could almost recant all the sarcasm I've written above [. . . .]

NOTE

1. See, for a very different account of this event, Christopher Hassall, *Rupert Brooke: A Biography*, Faber & Faber, 1972, 376–80.

Bibliography

INDIVIDUAL POETS

Armstrong, Martin. *Thirty New Poems*. London: Chapman & Hall, 1918.

——. *The Buzzards and Other Poems*, London: Martin Secker, 1921.

Baring, Maurice. *Poems, 1914–1919*. London: Martin Secker, 1920.

Beckh, Harold. *Swallows in Storm and Sunlight*. London: Chapman & Hall, 1917.

Békássy, Ferenc. *Adriatica and Other Poems*. London: The Hogarth Press, 1925.

Bendall, Frederic. *Front Line Lyrics*. London: Elkin Mathews, 1918.

Brooke, Rupert. *1914 and Other Poems*. London: Sidgwick & Jackson, 1915.

——. *Collected Poems*. London: Sidgwick & Jackson, 1918.

Brown, John. *Dies Heroica: War Poems: 1914–1918*. London: Hodder & Stoughton, 1918.

Bullett, Gerald. *Mice, and Other Poems*. Cambridge: Perkin Warbeck, 1921.

——. *Poems*. Cambridge: Cambridge University Press, 1949.

Cole, Margaret Postgate. *Poems; by Margaret Postgate*. London: Allen & Unwin, 1918.

Cooke, Greville. *Poems*. Oxford: Blackwell, 1933.

Day, Jeffery. *Poems and Rhymes*. London: Sidgwick & Jackson, 1919.

De Candole, Alec. *Poems*. Cambridge: Cambridge University Press, 1920.

Esdaile, Arundell. *Moments*. London: 1932.

Ewer, William. *Five Souls, and Other War-time Verses*. London: The Herald, 1917.

Fyson, Geoffrey. *The Survivors, and Other Poems*. London: Erskine Macdonald, 1919.

Haseler, Digby. *Verses From France to the Family*. London: Erskine Macdonald, 1919.

——. *Home-Made Verses*. Cambridge: Perkin Warbeck, 1921.

Head, Sir Henry. *Destroyers and Other Verses*. London: Milford, 1919.

Johnson, Donald. *Poems*. Cambridge: Cambridge University Press, 1919.

Macaulay, Dame Rose. *Three Days*. London: Constable, 1919.

——. *Poems of Today*. London: Sidgwick & Jackson, 1919.

Macleod, John. *Macedonian Measures and Others*. Cambridge: Cambridge University Press, 1919.

Milne, A. A. *The Sunny Side*. London: Methuen, 1921.

———. *For the Luncheon Interval: Cricket and Other Verses*. London: Methuen, 1925.

Monro, Harold. *Strange Meetings*. London: Poetry Bookshop, 1917.

———. *Collected Poems*. London: Cobden Sanderson, 1933.

Nicklin, John. *And They Went to War*. London: Sidgwick & Jackson, 1914.

Pemberton, V. T. *Reflections in Verse*. London: Grant Richards, 1919.

Sassoon, Siegfried. *The Old Huntsman*. London: Heinemann, 1917.

———. *Counter-Attack*. London: Heinemann, 1918. *War Poems*. London: Heinemann, 1919.

———. *Collected Poems*. London: Faber, 1947.

———. *The War Poems*. London: Faber & Faber, 1983.

Seaman, Sir Owen. *War-time Verses*. London: Constable, 1915.

———. *From the Home Front*. London: Constable, 1918.

Shanks, Edward. *Poems*. London: Sidgwick & Jackson, 1916.

———. *The Queen of China*. London: Martin Secker, 1919.

———. *Poems, 1912–1932*. London: Macmillan, 1933.

———. *The Man from Flanders, and Other Poems*. London: St. Clements Press, 1940.

Shove, Fredegond. *Dreams and Journeys*. Oxford: Blackwell, 1918.

———. *Poems*. Cambridge: Cambridge University Press, 1956.

Sidgwick, Frank. *Some Verse*. London: Sidgwick & Jackson, 1915.

———. *More Verse*. London: Sidgwick & Jackson, 1921.

Simpson, Henry Lamont. *Moods and Tenses*. London: Erskine Macdonald, 1919.

Sorley, Charles Hamilton. *Marlborough and Other Poems*. Cambridge: Cambridge University Press, 1916.

———. *The Poems and Selected Letters of Charles Hamilton Sorley*. Blackness Press, 1978.

———. *The Collected Poems*. London: Cecil Woolf, 1985.

Squire, Sir John Collings. *The Survival of the Fittest, and Other Poems*. London: Allen & Unwin, 1916.

———. *Collected Poems*. London: Macmillan, 1959.

Tillyard, Aelfrida. *The Garden and the Fire*. Cambridge: Heffer, 1916.

Tomlinson, Albert E. *Candour*. London: Elkin Mathews, 1922.

Wallace, Kathleen. *Lost City: Verses*. Cambridge: Heffer, 1918.

Williams, Iolo A. *Poems*. London: Methuen, 1915. *New Poems* London: Methuen, 1919.

Young, E. Hilton. *A Muse at Sea: Verses*. London: Sidgwick & Jackson, 1919.

Young, Geoffrey W. *From the Trenches*. London: T. Fisher Unwin, 1914.

———. *Bolts from the Blues: Rhymes*. Gorizia, 1917.

———. *Freedom*. London: Smith Elder (John Murray, 1914).

ANTHOLOGIES

Adcock, A. St. J., ed. *For Remembrance: Soldier Poets Who Have Fallen in the War*. London: Hodder & Stoughton, 1920.

Andrews, C. E., ed. *From the Front: Trench Poetry*. New York: Appleton, 1918.

Black, E. L. ed. *1914–1918 in Poetry: An Anthology*. London: London University Press, 1970.

Brereton, F., ed. *An Anthology of War Poems*. London: Collins, 1930.

Clarke, G. H., ed. *A Treasury of War Poetry*. London: Hodder & Stoughton, 1919.

Cross, T., ed. *The Lost Voices of World War I*. London: Bloomsbury, 1988.

Cunliffe, J.W., ed. *Poems of the Great War*. New York: Macmillan, 1916.

Davison, E., ed. *Cambridge Poets, 1914–1920*. Cambridge: Heffer, 1920.

Dickinson, P., ed. *Soldiers' Verse*. London: Muller, 1945.

Edwards, M. C., and M. Booth, eds. *The Fiery Cross: An Anthology*. London: Grant Richards, 1915.

Elliott, H. B., ed. *Lest We Forget: An Anthology*. London: Jarrolds, 1915.

Forshaw, C. F., ed. *One Hundred of the Best Poems on the European War*. London: Elliott Stock, 1915.

Gardner, B., ed. *Up the Line to Death*. London: Methuen, 1964.

Hibberd, D., and J. Onions, eds. *Poetry of the Great War: An Anthology*. London: Macmillan, 1986.

Hussey, M., ed. *Poetry of the First World War: An Anthology*. London: Longmans, 1967.

Khan, N., ed. *Not With Loud Grieving: Women's Verse of the Great War: An Anthology*. Lahore: Polymer Publicatons, 1994.

Kyle, G., ed. *Soldier Poets: Songs of the Fighting Men*. London: Erskine Macdonald, 1916.

———. *Soldier Poets: More Songs by the Fighting Men*. London: Erskine Macdonald, 1917.

Lloyd, B., ed. *Poems Written during the Great War, 1914–1918: An Anthology*. London: Allen & Unwin, 1918.

———. *The Paths of Glory: A Collection of Poems Written during the War*. London: Allen & Unwin, 1919.

Nichols, R., ed. *Anthology of War Poetry, 1914–1918*. London: Nicholson & Watson, 1943.

Osborn, E. B., ed. *The Muse in Arms*. London: Murray, 1917.

Parsons, I. M., ed. *Men Who March Away: Poems of the First World War: An Anthology*. London: Chatto & Windus, 1965.

Pocock, G. N., ed. *Modern Poetry*. London: Dent, 1920.

Powell, A., ed. *A Deep Cry*. Aberporth: Palladour Books, 1993.

———. *The Fierce Light*. Aberporth: Palladour Books, 1996.

Reilly, C., ed. *Scars Upon My Heart: Women's Poetry and Verse of the First World War*. London: Virago, 1980.

Royle, T., ed. *In Flanders Fields: Scottish Poetry and Prose of the First World War*. Edinburgh: Mainstream Publishing, 1990.

Silkin, J., ed. *The Penguin Book of First World War Poetry*. London: Penguin Books, 1979

Stephen, M., ed. *Never Such Innocence: A New Anthology of Great War Verse*. London: Buchan & Enright, 1988.

Taylor, M., ed. *Lads: Love Poetry of the Trenches*. London: Constable, 1989.

Trotter, J. T., ed. *Valour and Vision: Poems of the War, 1914–1918*. London: Martin Hopkinson & Co. Ltd., 1920.

Walkerdine, W. E., ed. *Poems of the Great War*. 1916.

BIBLIOGRAPHY

Reilly, C. W. *English Poetry of the First World War: A Bibliography*. London: George Prior Publications, 1978.

CRITICISM, BIOGRAPHY, HISTORY, ETC.

Bergonzi, B., *Heroes' Twilight*. London: Constable, 1965.

Blunden, E. *War Poets: 1914–1918*. London: Longmans, Green & Co., 1953.

Brooke, C. N. L. *A History of the University of Cambridge, vol. III, 1870–1990*. Cambridge: Cambridge University Press, 1997.

Caesar, A. *Taking it Like a Man: Suffering, Sexuality and the War Poets: Brooke, Sassoon, Owen, Graves*. Manchester: Manchester University Press, 1993.

Campbell, P. *Siegfried Sassoon: A Study of the War Poetry*. Jefferson: McFarland & Co., 1999.

Chainey, G. *A Literary History of Cambridge*. Cambridge: The Pevensey Press, 1985.

Copp, M., ed. *From Emmanuel to the Somme: The War Writings of A.E. Tomlinson*. Cambridge: The Lutterworth Press, 1997.

Crawford, F. D. *British Poets of the Great War*. London: Associated University Presses, 1988.

Deacon, R. *The Cambridge Apostles*. London: Robert Royce Ltd., 1985.

Delany, P. *The Neo-Pagans: Friendship and Love in the Rupert Brooke Circle*. London: Macmillan, 1987.

Eksteins, M. *Rites of Spring: The Great War and the Birth of the Modern Age*. London: Bantam Press, 1989.

Field, F. *British and French Writers of the First World War*. Cambridge: Cambridge University Press, 1991.

Fussell, P. *The Great War and Modern Memory*. Oxford: Oxford University Press, 1975.

Hassall, C. *Rupert Brooke: A Biography*. London: Faber & Faber, 1964.

Hastings, M. *The Handsomest Young Man in England: Rupert Brooke*. London: Michael Joseph, 1967.

Henderson, R.J. *A History of King's College Choir School*. Cambridge, 1981.

Hibberd, D. *Wilfred Owen: The Last Year*. London: Constable, 1992.

Hibberd, D., ed. *Poetry of the First World War: A Casebook*. London: Macmillan, 1981.

Hynes, S. *A War Imagined: The First World War and English Culture*. London: The Bodley Head, 1990.

Johnston, J. H. *English Poetry of the First World War: A Study of the Evolution of Lyric and Narrative Form*. Princeton: Princeton University Press, 1964.

Jones, A. R. *The Life and Opinions of T. E. Hulme*. London: Gollancz, 1960.

Jones N. *Rupert Brooke, Life, Death and Myth*. London: Richard Cohen Books, 1999.

Keynes, G., ed. *The Letters of Rupert Brooke*. London: Faber & Faber 1968.

Leedham-Green, E. *A Concise History of the University of Cambridge*. Cambridge: Cambridge University Press, 1996.

Lehmann, J. *Rupert Brooke: His Life and Legend*. London: Weidenfeld and Nicolson Ltd., 1980.

Marsland, E. A. *The Nation's Cause: French, English and German Poetry of the First World War*. London: Routledge, 1991.

Moeyes, P. *Siegfried Sassoon: Scorched Glory: A Critical Study*. London: Macmillan, 1997.

Pearsall, R. B. *Rupert Brooke: The Man and the Poet*. Amsterdam: Rodopi, 1974.

Quinn, P. *The Great War and the Missing Muse: The Early Writings of Robert Graves and Siegfried Sassoon*. London: Associated University Presses, 1994.

Read, M. *Forever England: The Life of Rupert Brooke*. Edinburgh: Mainstream Publishing, 1997.

Roberts, J. S. *Siegfried Sassoon*. London: Richard Cohen Books, 1999.

Roucoux, M., ed. *English Literature of the Great War Revisited*. University of Picardy, 1986.

Silkin, J. *Out of Battle: The Poetry of the Great War*. Oxford: Oxford University Press, 1972.

Stephen, M. *The Price of Pity: Poetry, History and Myth in the Great War*. London: Leo Cooper, 1996.

Sternlicht, S. *Siegfried Sassoon*. Twayne, 1993.

Swann. T. B. *The Ungirt Runner: Charles Hamilton Sorley, Poet of World War I*. Archon, 1965.

Thorpe, M. *Siegfried Sassoon: A Critical Study*. Oxford: Oxford University Press, 1967.

Thwaite, A. *A. A. Milne : His Life*. London: Faber & Faber, 1990.

Turner, J. F. *Rupert Brooke: The Splendour and the Pain*. London: Breese Books, 1992.

Wilson, J. M. *Charles Hamilton Sorley: A Biography*. London: Cecil Woolf, 1985.

———. *The Collected Letters of Charles Hamilton Sorley*. London: Cecil Woolf, 1985.

———. *Siegfried Sassoon: The Making of a War Poet: A Biography*. London: Duckworth, 1998.

Index of Authors

Page references to the Introduction (pp. 23–63), Biographical Notes (pp. 235–49), and Appendices (pp. 250–53) are given in italic.

Index of Titles

Index of First Lines